london

Hello.

C000213522

Editor Nikki Wicks
Senior Editor David Edwards
Art Director Ben Martin
Managing Editor Kevin McCreeth
Sub-editors Helen Morgan,
Charlie Ghagan, Anna Downing,
Rosanna Farrell, Dan Blows, Paul
Fearnley, James Charlton, Edward Craig,
Joe Miller, Martin Boon
Associate Editor Steve Landells
Staff Writer Vithushan Ehantharajah
Designers Rebecca Studd, Chris Barker
Picture Editors Dominique Campbell,
Jenny Quiggin, Richard Lawrence
Contributors Karien Jonckheere,
Valerie Siebert, Cath Millman
Photographers Getty Images; Press
Association Images; BBC Sport's Frank Keogh
Commercial Director Mark Hanrahan
Sales Manager Stuart Staves
Head of Production Gary Charlton
Group Production Manager Jane Grist
Senior Production Controller Iain Green
Repro Haymarket Prepress: Darren Jones,
Carl Price, Ricky McGrath, Bob Wayman
Printed by Wyndeham Heron
Printed on Galerie Art supplied by
Antalis McNaughton
Senior Account Manager Julia Saunders
Account Manager Ian Paynton
Account Executive Joshua Kanter
Group Art Director Martin Tullett
Director Cormac Bourne
Director, Management Accounts
Mark Jeffries
MD Haymarket Network Andrew Taplin
Editorial Director Simon Kanter
Creative Director Paul Harpin
Chief Executive Kevin Costello
Executive Chairman Rupert Heseltine
**The London Organising Committee of
the Olympic Games and Paralympic
Games Ltd (LOCOG)**
Chair Sebastian Coe KBE
CEO Paul Deighton
Also for LOCOG Laura Turner Laing,
John Heyes, John Murray, Rob Findlay

Published under licence from London 2012
by Haymarket Media Group, Teddington
Studios, Broom Road, Teddington, Middlesex
TW11 9BE, UK. Telephone +44 (0) 20
8267 5000. Reprinting in whole or in part is
forbidden except with the prior permission of
the publisher. Due care is taken to ensure that
the content of this magazine is fully accurate,
but the publisher and printer cannot accept
liability for errors and omissions. Views
expressed by contributors are not necessarily
shared by LOCOG. London 2012 emblems ©
The London Organising Committee of the
Olympic Games and Paralympic Games Ltd
(LOCOG) 2007. London 2012 Pictograms ©
LOCOG 2009. London 2012 mascots ©
LOCOG 2009 – 2010 All rights reserved.

Welcome to the Official Review of the London 2012 Olympic Games. We are all still catching our breath after the most amazing 16 days of sport and spectacle. The Opening Ceremony, Danny Boyle's riotous celebration of all things British, set the standard for London 2012 – brilliantly organised, feelgood and fun – and the sport that followed has scarcely paled in comparison. The athletes of Great Britain and Northern Ireland have had their best Olympic Games for 104 years, and those of us who have watched from the venues and further afield have marvelled at their performances. In the Official Review we relive the drama and joy of each day, list every medal winner and show where each member of Team GB finished. In short, it's London 2012 in all its glory. Our glorious Games.

David Edwards
Senior Editor

Contents

'For me it was a wonderful feeling, I was slightly nervous, but that cheer that I got (from the crowd) made all the jitters go away'
Usain Bolt on the build-up to the 100m final

'I can't believe this has happened to me, I'm peaking at the right time and it's all thanks to the coaches, and the support of the crowd and my family'
Laura Trott on her Track Cycling Omnium victory

Our glorious

'I started sailing in Cornwall as an eight-year-old in a duffle coat and wellies and now I'm standing here. You never know what can happen'
Ben Ainslie gives his reaction to becoming the most decorated Olympic sailor in history

'I came into the competition in good shape, the best shape of my life. I had the belief that I could do it. The crowd lift you so much, they support you so much'
Jess Ennis on her victory in the women's Heptathlon

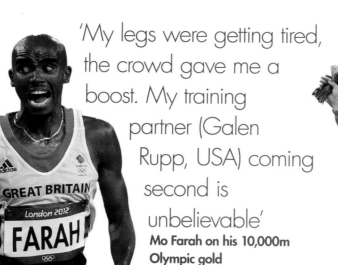

'My legs were getting tired, the crowd gave me a boost. My training partner (Galen Rupp, USA) coming second is unbelievable'
Mo Farah on his 10,000m Olympic gold

'I'm in shock. I'm trying to take it all in, but this is surreal. I always wanted to win gold in front of my home crowd. It's just the most amazing feeling'
Sir Chris Hoy on becoming the most successful Briton in Olympic history

Games

'It's been a long, long wait. It's not been painful, I've had a great few years. This is the culmination of a lot of hard work'
Katherine Grainger on winning gold after three Olympic silver medals

'Every Olympics has got better and better. The people have been great, the food is better. It was fun'
Michael Phelps on London 2012

Off with a bang
The Opening Ceremony for the
London 2012 Olympic Games
kicks off with spectacular fireworks
at the Olympic Stadium

A night to remember

Danny Boyle's witty and ambitious Opening Ceremony provided the watching world with a dramatic and spectacular account of Britain's cultural history. Here, we look back at some of the most memorable moments, including cameos from Bradley Wiggins, David Beckham and Mr Bean

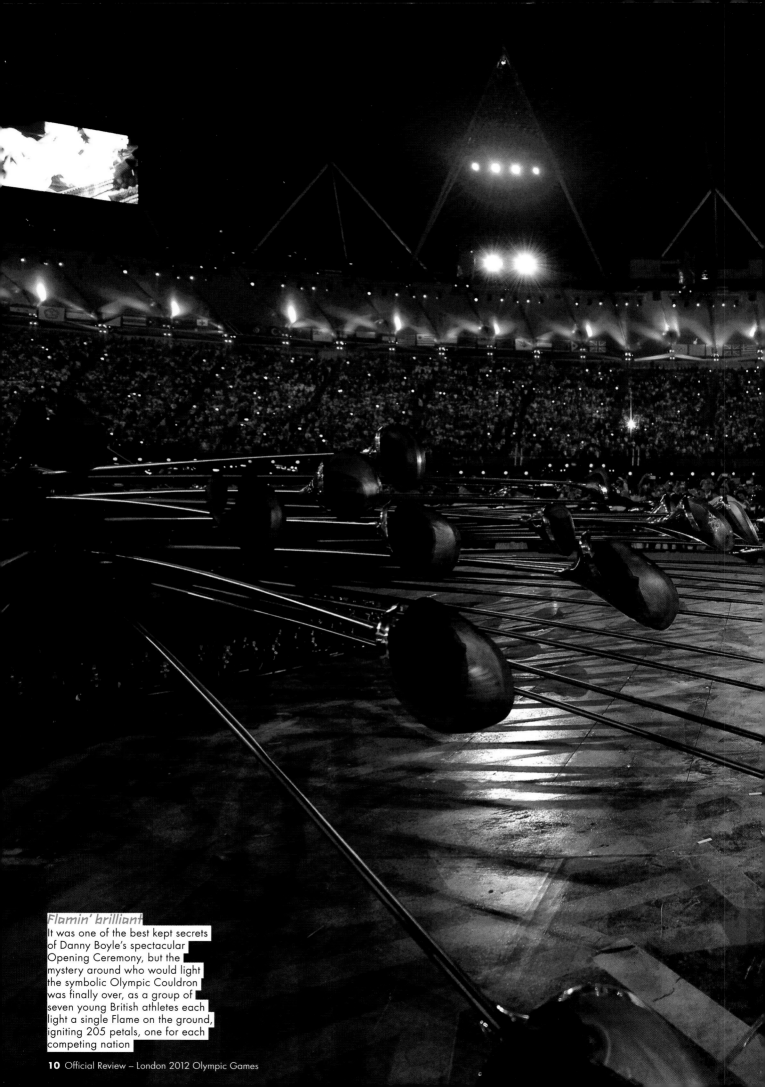

Flamin' brilliant

It was one of the best kept secrets of Danny Boyle's spectacular Opening Ceremony, but the mystery around who would light the symbolic Olympic Couldron was finally over, as a group of seven young British athletes each light a single Flame on the ground, igniting 205 petals, one for each competing nation

'I have great admiration for my coach... good teamwork is the key to being successful'

ROVSHAN BAYRAM
AZERBAIJAN
Greco-Roman Wrestling

NAIR ALMEIDA
ANGOLA
Handball

MOHAMMED AHMED ALI GHARIB
UAE
Football

We salute you

As proud sponsors of athletes from all over the globe, BP says congratulations to its London 2012 athletes

During the London 2012 Olympic Games, the UK was the centre of the sporting universe. While London played Host City, BP's involvement reached beyond national borders, and its impact was felt in all corners of the globe.

Working to build a lasting legacy, BP saw London 2012 as an opportunity to help the local communities in which it does business. It is proud to have supported a number of outstanding athletes from all over the world – from Angola and Azerbaijan to Egypt and the USA – as they fought for positions on the podium.

BP congratulates all their athletes who competed in the London 2012 Olympic Games. Even after the Closing Ceremonies, BP's work will continue, supporting athletes and their communities across the globe.

'I can't believe I did it.'
REBECCA SONI
USA
Swimming

'It was a great pleasure to represent my country in the London 2012 Olympic Games. It is an honour for me.'
METE BINAY
TURKEY
Weightlifting

NJISANE PHILLIP
TRINIDAD AND TOBAGO
Track Cycling

'It's been a whirlwind and I'm just blown away.'

JESSICA ENNIS
GREAT BRITAIN
Heptathlon

VARLAM LIPARTELIANI
GEORGIA
Judo

TAREK YEYHA
EGYPT
Weightlifting

bp
official partner

Visit bp.com/london2012

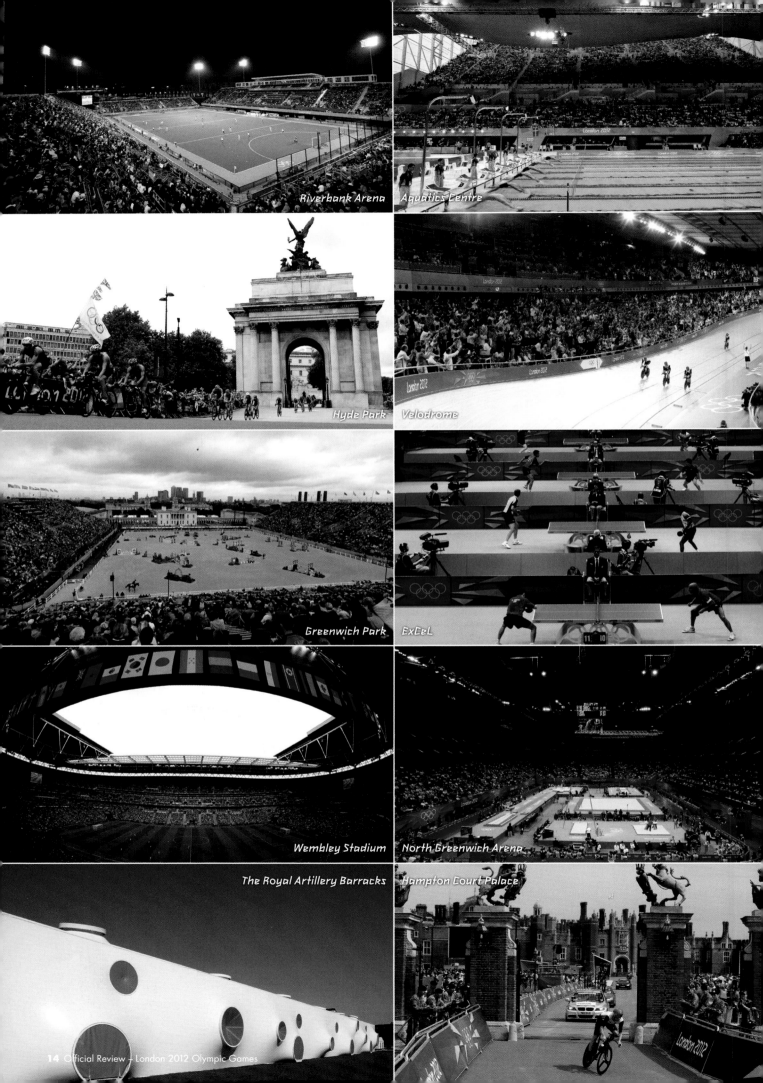

Riverbank Arena

Aquatics Centre

Hyde Park

Velodrome

Greenwich Park

ExCeL

Wembley Stadium

North Greenwich Arena

The Royal Artillery Barracks

Hampton Court Palace

Wimbledon

St. James' Park

Basketball Arena

The Mall

Olympic Stadium

Eton Dorney

Lord's Cricket Ground

Copper Box

City of Coventry Stadium

Lee Valley White Water Centre

DON'T LOOK AT THE LEGS. LOOK AT THE RECORDS.

Tickets for the London 2012 Paralympic Games are on sale now
www.tickets.london2012.com

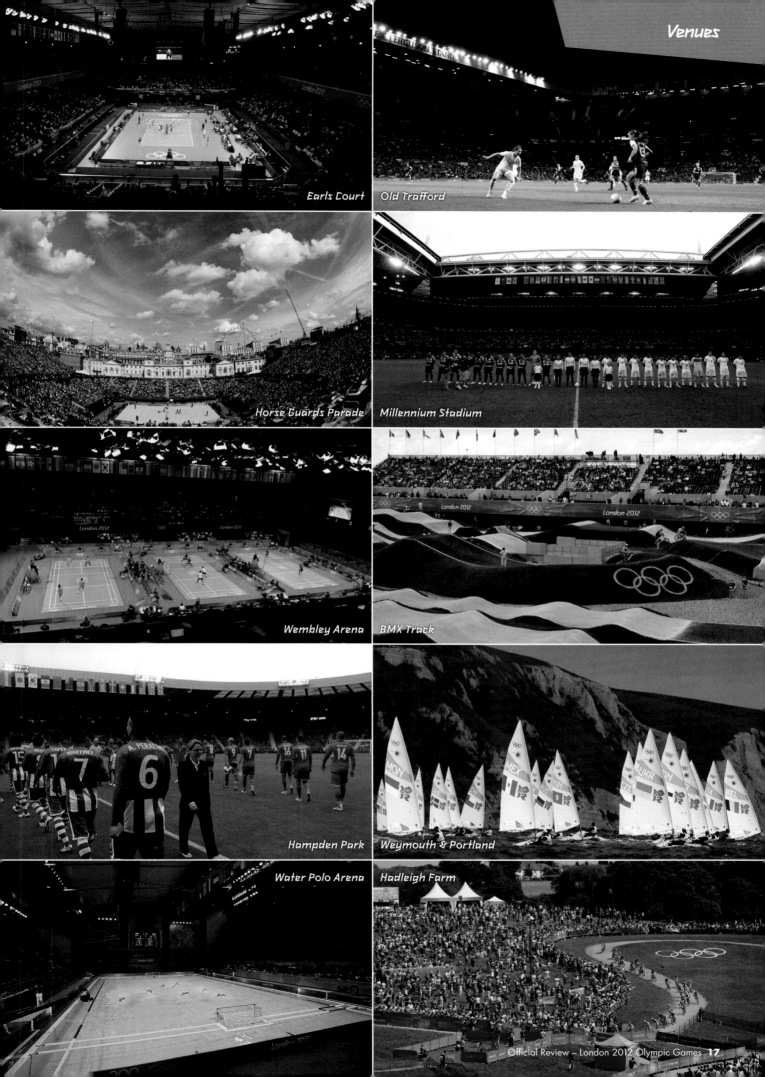

Earls Court

Old Trafford

Horse Guards Parade

Millennium Stadium

Wembley Arena

BMX Track

Hampden Park

Weymouth & Portland

Water Polo Arena

Hadleigh Farm

Park life

**BP showed Olympic Park visitors
how they helped to fuel the Games**

E veryone who visited the Olympic Park will never
forget it. And that's not just down to the sports. Thanks
to BP, every spectator at London 2012 had the
chance to learn about the journey of the energy we all
rely on and take part in an exciting world record attempt.

Using cutting-edge technology, BP's Walk in the Olympic
Park showcase inspired spectators and athletes to go for
gold with their energy usage. A 15-minute film, 'Fuelling
the Future', immersed visitors in the world of BP technology,
showing how they helped fuel London 2012. Presented by
athletes and projected onto a huge 360-degree rotating
screen, the amazing story motivated people to sign up to
BP's Target Neutral programme: visitors became part of an
exciting world record attempt, which aimed to offset the
largest number of spectator journeys to one event, for free.
And thanks to over 400,000 visitors, athletes and
journalists, the Games set a new world record.

It didn't end there. Anyone who strolled along the
two-mile Walk in the Olympic Park route, which explained
how sustainability is key to London 2012, was unable to
miss one final piece of BP technology: a giant periscope
made of 90 percent recycled steel from East End foundries.
Sitting inside it, visitors posed for free pictures in front of a
unique view of the Stadium, getting a lasting memory of an
amazing day out.

The Olympic Journey: The Story of the Olympic Games

Building on its 30-year support of arts
and culture in the UK, BP supported a
host of cultural events, as Premier Partner
of the Cultural Olympiad and London
2012 Festival. One of the highlights was
the innovative collaboration between the
Royal Opera House, the Olympic
Museum and BP.

Telling the Olympic story through the
achievements of ancient and modern
Olympians, the free exhibition contained
fascinating artefacts never seen before in
London – from all the summer Olympic
Games medals since 1896 to every
summer Olympic Torch since 1936.
Visitors were also treated to films about
16 of London 2012's athletes and a
projection of an ancient Greek chariot
race, recalling the interesting origins of
the Olympic Games.

official partner

Visit bptargetneutral.com

Official London 2012 Programmes
The ultimate souvenir

A to Z of sports

Top medal hopefuls

Exclusive pictures and interviews

Striking athlete and venue images

Unparalleled behind-the-scenes information

Buy at london2012.com/shop and other good retailers

Only £10

16 Days

The best pictures and stories
from the London 2012 Olympic Games

Day 1

Surprise!

The script has been written. Less than 12 hours after the Opening Ceremony has celebrated all that's best about Britain, Mark Cavendish is going to show the world what's great about British sport on Day 1 of London 2012.

Only six days earlier Cavendish had proved himself the best sprinter in cycling to win the final stage of the Tour de France. But, even with the help of Tour winner Bradley Wiggins in Team GB, Cavendish can not reproduce the heroics of the Champs-Elysées on the streets of London and Surrey and Alexandr Vinokurov of Kazakhstan wins the head to head sprint to take gold.

As if that's not surprise enough, Michael Phelps then produces the shock of Day 1. Being beaten by his arch-rival Ryan Lochte in the men's 400m Individual Medley is not in itself a shock but to finish out of the medals – in fourth place – is almost a first. Only once before has Phelps failed to win a medal in an Olympic Swimming event.

Ryan Lochte of the USA celebrates winning gold after the Victory Ceremony for the men's 400m Individual Medley

Siling Yi of China wins the first gold medal of the Games – the women's 10m Air Rifle at The Royal Artillery Barracks – by edging out Poland's Sylwia Bogacka

Korea win a medal in the men's Team Archery event for the fifth Olympic Games in a row, following a 224-219 victory over Mexico in the bronze medal match

Russian Fed's Arsen Galstyan hails his victory over Japan's Hiroaki Hiraoka to win gold in the men's Judo -60kg category

China's Siling Yi beams broadly at The Royal Artillery Barracks after winning the first gold medal of the London 2012 Olympic Games

Table Tennis

Paul Drinkhall and his girlfriend **Joanna Parker** enjoy double success – both British players making it through their first-round matches at ExCeL

Rowing

WORLD RECORD (men's Pair) New Zealand's **Hamish Bond** and **Eric Murray** take a huge six seconds out of James Cracknell and Matthew Pinsent's men's Pair Rowing world record with a time of 6:08.50

Weightlifting

Hiromi Miyake of Japan wins a silver medal in the women's 48kg weight division to join her father and uncle as an Olympic medallist

Michele Frangilli shoots a perfect 10 with the final arrow to help Italy to an epic 219-218 defeat of the USA in the men's Team Archery Competition final

Quote of the day

'I felt like a movie star! Now I've got the gold medal I feel very happy and very excited. I almost cried'

Shooter Siling Yi of China on winning the first gold medal of London 2012

★
Star of the day
Ryan Lochte

It's advantage Lochte after Day 1 at the Aquatics Centre, in his rivalry with compatriot Michael Phelps. Lochte picks up the first London 2012 Swimming gold medal on offer, winning the men's 400m Individual Medley convincingly.

Judo

Great Britain's **Ashley McKenzie** is knocked out of the men's Judo -60kg competition after losing to Hiroaki Hiraoka of Japan in the last 32 at ExCeL

Swimming

Australia take gold and end the winning streak of defending Olympic champions Netherlands in the women's 4 x 100m Freestyle Relay, in 3:33.15

Yang Sun wins China's first gold medal in men's Swimming as he triumphs in the men's 400m Freestyle with an Olympic record 3:40.14

Day 1, 28 July

Who won the medals today

Morning
Shooting
Women's 10m Air Rifle
- Siling Yi (CHN)............................502.9
- Sylwia Bogacka (POL)...................502.2
- Dan Yu (CHN) 501.5

Afternoon
Shooting
Men's 10m Air Pistol
- Jongoh Jin (KOR)............................688.2
- Luca Tesconi (ITA) 685.8
- Andrija Zlatic (SRB) 685.2

Afternoon
Cycling – Road
Men's Road Race
- Alexandr Vinokurov (KAZ) 5:45:57
- Rigoberto Uran Uran (COL)..........5:45:57
- Alexander Kristoff (NOR).............5:46:05

Afternoon
Judo
Women's -48kg
- Sarah Menezes (BRA) 011
- Alina Dumitru (ROU)........................0001
- Charline van Snick (BEL) 0011-0002
- Eva Csernoviczki (HUN) 1001-0001

Afternoon
Judo
Men's -60 kg
- Arsen Galstyan (RUS) 100
- Hiroaki Hiraoka (JPN) 000
- Felipe Kitadai (BRA) 0011-000
- Rishod Sobirov (UZB)...............010-0003

Afternoon
Weightlifting
Women's 48kg
- Mingjuan Wang (CHN)................. 205kg
- Hiromi Miyake (JPN) 197kg
- Chun Hwa Ryang (PRK) 192kg

Afternoon
Archery
Men's Team Competition
- Italy 219
- USA 218
- Korea 224-219

Evening
Swimming
Men's 400m Individual Medley
- Ryan Lochte (USA)....................... 4:05.18
- Thiago Pereira (BRA) 4:08.86
- Kosuke Hagino (JPN)................... 4:08.94

Evening
Swimming
Men's 400m Freestyle
- Yang Sun (CHN) ....3:40.14 (OR)
- Tae-Hwan Park (KOR)..................3:42.06
- Peter Vanderkaay (USA) 3:44.69

Evening
Fencing
Women's Individual Foil
- Elisa Di Francisca (ITA) 12
- Arianna Errigo (ITA) 11
- Valentina Vezzali (ITA) 13-12

Evening
Swimming
Women's 400m Individual Medley
- Shiwen Ye (CHN)...............4:28.43 (WR)
- Elizabeth Beisel (USA) 4:31.27
- Xuanxu Li (CHN) 4:32.91

Evening
Swimming
Women's 4 x 100m Freestyle Relay
- Australia .... 3:33.15 (OR)
- Netherlands 3:33.79
- USA.. 3:34.24

9,660,000

Total number of worldwide Twitter mentions of the Opening Ceremony from the start to the end of its broadcast in the USA

A frustrating day for Team GB in the men's Cycling Road Race ends with pre-race favourite Mark Cavendish finishing 29th

011

Sarah Menezes' score in the women's Judo -48kg category to win Brazil's first Olympic gold medal in Judo since 1992, when Rogerio Sampaio Cardoso won gold in the men's -66kg

5

Hiromi Miyake wins Japan's first Olympic medal in women's Weightlifting (silver), but it was the fifth to be won by her family. Father Yoshiyuki (bronze) and uncle Yoshinobu (gold) shared the podium in the men's 69kg event at the 1968 Olympic Games. Her uncle also won two other Olympic medals

4:28.43

Shiwen Ye of China becomes the first woman to break a Swimming world record after the high-tech suit ban with a blisteringly quick 4:28.43 to take gold in the 400m Individual Medley ahead of world champion Elizabeth Beisel of the USA

Chun Hwa Ryang's bronze medal in the women's Weightlifting 48kg category is the tenth Olympic medal for DPR Korea in this sport

4 Italy won the women's Individual Foil for the fourth consecutive Olympic Games to set a new record for consecutive wins by any country in any women's Fencing event

Italy's Elisa Di Francisca (left) wins gold in the women's Individual Foil after defeating compatriot Arianna Errigo in extra time at ExCeL

Medal table

1	China	4	0	2	6
2	Italy	2	2	1	5
3	USA	1	2	2	5
4	Brazil	1	1	1	3
4	Korea	1	1	1	3
6	Australia	1	0	0	1
6	Kazakhstan	1	0	0	1
6	Russian Federation	1	0	0	1
9	Japan	0	2	1	3
10	Colombia	0	1	0	1
10	Netherlands	0	1	0	1
10	Poland	0	1	0	1
10	Romania	0	1	0	1
14	Belgium	0	0	1	1
14	Hungary	0	0	1	1
14	Norway	0	0	1	1
14	DPR Korea	0	0	1	1
14	Serbia	0	0	1	1
14	Uzbekistan	0	0	1	1

38 years 316 days

The age of Kazakhstan's Alexandr Vinokurov, winner of the gold medal in the men's Cycling Road Race – making him the oldest gold medallist in Olympic Road Cycling. He surpasses the record of Jeannie Longo-Ciprelli of France, who was 37 years and 264 days when she won the women's Road Race at Atlanta 1996.

Mingjuan Wang of China hoists the winning lift in the women's Weightlifting 48kg category at ExCeL

Her Majesty The Queen meets one of the taller members of Team GB during a tour of the Olympic Village

Here comes the rain

After some glorious days of sunshine in London, Day 2 brings the rain. A day after the disappointment for the men, Team GB women has the chance to secure Great Britain's first medal in the Cycling Road Race. And in a rain-soaked finish on The Mall, Lizzie Armitstead sprints to win a silver medal, just behind Dutch superstar Marianne Vos.

The water appears to be a good omen for Great Britain on Day 2, as Rebecca Adlington finishes strongly to win bronze in the pool in the 400m Freestyle behind Camille Muffat of France and USA's Allison Schmitt.

There is a close shave in the Fencing competition at ExCeL, as Aldo Montano, the Athens 2004 men's Individual Sabre champion, appears with the words 'God save the Queen' shaved into the back of his head. Montano, who fails to make the semi-finals in London, later reveals that his wacky hair-do is in honour of his grandfather, who claimed silver in the same event at London 1948.

Day 2

Britain's Lizzie Armitstead cannot quite catch Marianne Vos of Netherlands, who wins the women's Cycling Road Race on The Mall. Armitstead takes silver and Britain's first medal of the Games

Swimming

South Africa's **Cameron van der Burgh** smashes the world record in the men's 100m Breaststroke final to claim his country's first gold of the Games with a time of 58.46 seconds

Archery

Korea secure a seventh successive Olympic women's Team Archery title as China miss out on gold by just one point after 24 arrows – it's the third successive Games they have won silver

Gymnastics

The youngest – and shortest – member of Team GB, **Rebecca Tunney** qualifies as the top Briton for the final of the women's Individual All-Around Competition final

Rebecca Adlington produces a typical strong finish to claim Britain's first medal in the pool – bronze in the 400m Freestyle behind Camille Muffat of France and USA's Allison Schmitt

Quote of the day

'I seem to be breaking a lot of records when it comes to age. I am pleased to have got another one'

Ryan Giggs, on breaking an 88-year-old record to become the oldest men's goalscorer at an Olympic Games Football tournament, at 38 years of age

Ryan Giggs scores the opening goal for Team GB in the Group A Football match against United Arab Emirates. The match finished 3-1 to Great Britain

Britain's women's Lightweight Double Sculls pair, **Katherine Copeland** and **Sophie Hosking** dominate their heat at Eton Dorney

Team GB women's Beach Volleyball pair **Shauna Mullin** and **Zara Dampney** kick off their Olympic medal bid with a win over Canada

France reverse the result from Beijing 2008 after edging out the USA in the men's 4 x 100m Freestyle Relay final and winning the gold medal

Great Britain's Mark Hunter and Zac Purchase cruise into the men's Lightweight Double Sculls semi-finals at Eton Dorney

Paul Drinkhall of Great Britain serves in a surprise victory over Singapore's Yang Zi at ExCeL in the men's Single Table Tennis competition

★
Star of the day
Kimberly Rhode

China's Minxia Wu and Zi He dominate the women's Synchronised 3m Springboard event to win the first Diving gold medal of the Games

The shooter becomes the first American to win individual medals at five consecutive Olympic Games, after securing a gold medal in the women's Skeet at The Royal Artillery Barracks. Rhode overcame a rocky build-up to her London 2012 bid after flight cancellations forced her to miss her team training camp...and her puppy ate her plane ticket.

Weightlifting

Judo

Gymnastics – Artistic

Zulfiya Chinshanlo of Kazakhstan sets a new world record of 131kg in the clean and jerk en route to taking gold in the women's 53kg Weightlifting division

Judoka **Kum Ae An** of DPR Korea turns her Beijing 2008 silver medal into a gold after defeating Yanet Bermoy Acosta of Cuba in the final of the -52kg category

USA women's Artistic Gymnastics team dominate the qualifiers, entering the Team Competition final on top as well as securing no fewer than eight Individual final slots

Day 2, 29 July

Who won the medals today

Afternoon
Shooting
Women's 10m Air Pistol
- Wenjun Guo (CHN) 488.1
- Celine Goberville (FRA) 486.6
- Olena Kostevych (UKR).....................486.6

Afternoon
Shooting
Women's Skeet
- Kimberly Rhode (USA) 99
- Ning Wei (CHN) 91
- Danka Bartekova (SVK) 90

Afternoon
Diving
Women's Synchronised 3m Springboard
- Zi He/Minxia Wu (CHN)................ 346.20
- Kelci Bryant/Abigail Johnston (USA) . 321.90
- Jennifer Abel/Emilie Heymans (CAN).. 316.80

Afternoon
Cycling Road
Women's Road Race
- Marianne Vos (NED) 3:35.29
- Elizabeth Armitstead (GBR)............3:35.29
- Olga Zabelinskaya (RUS)...............3:35.31

Afternoon
Judo
Women's -52kg
- Kum Ae An (PRK) 001
- Yanet Bermoy Acosta (CUB) 000
- Rosalba Forciniti (ITA)............... 000-0001
- Priscilla Gneto (FRA)..................1012-0012

Afternoon
Judo
Men's -66kg
- Lasha Shavdatuashvili (GEO) 001
- Miklos Ungvari (HUN)...................... 0001
- Masashi Ebinuma (JPN) 110-0101
- Jun-Ho Cho (KOR) 000-0001

Afternoon
Weightlifting
Women's 53kg
- Zulfiya Chinshanlo (KAZ)...........226kg (OR)
- Shu-Ching Hsu (TPE)........................219kg
- Cristina Iovu (MDA)..........................219kg

Afternoon
Archery
Women's Team Competition
- Korea 210
- China 209
- Japan 209-207

Evening
Fencing
Men's Individual Sabre
- Aron Szilagyi (HUN) 15
- Diego Occhiuzzi (ITA) 8
- Nikolay Kovalev (RUS)......................15-10

Evening
Swimming
Women's 100m Butterfly
- Dana Vollmer (USA) .... 55.98 (WR)
- Ying Lu (CHN) 56.87
- Alicia Coutts (AUS) 56.94

Evening
Swimming
Men's 100m Breaststroke
- Cameron van der Burgh (RSA)... 58.46 (WR)
- Christian Sprenger (AUS) 58.93
- Brendan Hansen (USA)......................59.49

Evening
Weightlifting
Men's 56 kg
- Yun Chol Om (PRK) ....293kg (OR)
- Jingbiao Wu (CHN) 289kg
- Valentin Hristov (AZE).......................286kg

Evening
Swimming
Women's 400m Freestyle
- Camille Muffat (FRA) .... 4:01.45 (OR)
- Allison Schmitt (USA).....................4:01.77
- Rebecca Adlington (GBR) 4:03.01

Evening
Swimming
Men's 4 x 100m Freestyle Relay
- France 3:09.93
- USA 3:10.38
- Russia 3:11.41

Zulfiya Chinshanlo is the youngest women's Weightlifting champion in Olympic history after she won Kazakhstan's first Olympic gold medal in women's Weightlifting

19 women's Weightlifting champion (19 years, four days) in Olympic history

10.7m

Watch Rebecca Adlington win bronze in the women's 400m Freestyle on T

22

At 22, Aron Szilagyi (Hungary) is the youngest gold medal winner in men's Individual Sabre in 116 years – Ioannis Georgiadis (GRE), also 22, won in 1896

3x3

Wu Minxia (CHN) becomes the first athlete to win the women's Synchronised 3m Springboard at three consecutive Olympic Games after claiming gold alongside team-mate He Zi

USA became the first country to reach 500 total medals in Olympic Games Swimming (men and women)

USA gymnasts **Alexandra Raisman** and **Gabrielle Douglas** qualify for the Individual All-Around Competition in second and third place respectively, unexpectedly edging out their fellow American, and reigning world champion, Jordyn Wieber

Aldo Montano finishes 11th in the Fencing Individual Sabre, with 'God save the Queen' shaved into the back of his head in honour of his grandfather, who won silver at London 1948

Medal table

1	China	6	4	2	12
2	USA	3	5	3	11
3	Italy	2	3	2	7
4	Korea	2	1	2	5
5	France	2	1	1	4
6	DPR Korea	2	0	1	3
7	Kazakhstan	2	0	0	2
8	Australia	1	1	1	3
8	Brazil	1	1	1	3
8	Hungary	1	1	1	3
11	Netherlands	1	1	0	2
12	Russian Federation	1	0	3	4
13	Georgia	1	0	0	1
13	South Africa	1	0	0	1
15	Japan	0	2	3	5
16	Great Britain	0	1	1	2
17	Colombia	0	1	0	1
17	Cuba	0	1	0	1
17	Poland	0	1	0	1
17	Romania	0	1	0	1
17	Taipei (Chinese Taipei)	0	1	0	1
22	Azerbaijan	0	0	1	1
22	Belgium	0	0	1	1
22	Canada	0	0	1	1
22	Republic of Moldova	0	0	1	1
22	Norway	0	0	1	1
22	Serbia	0	0	1	1
22	Slovakia	0	0	1	1
22	Ukraine	0	0	1	1
22	Uzbekistan	0	0	1	1

10 Million litres of water fill the Aquatics Centre at the Olympic Park and it takes 180,000 tiles to line both 50m pools and the 25m diving pool

0.21 Rebecca Adlington wins bronze in the women's 400m Freestyle with a time of 4:03:01. That's 0.21 seconds faster than her gold medal time at Beijing 2008

Niger's Hamadou Djibo Issaka is dubbed the 'Eric the Eel' of Rowing after inciting the crowd at Eton Dorney to rapturous applause after finishing last in the men's Single Sculls repechages, nearly 1min 40sec behind the race winner

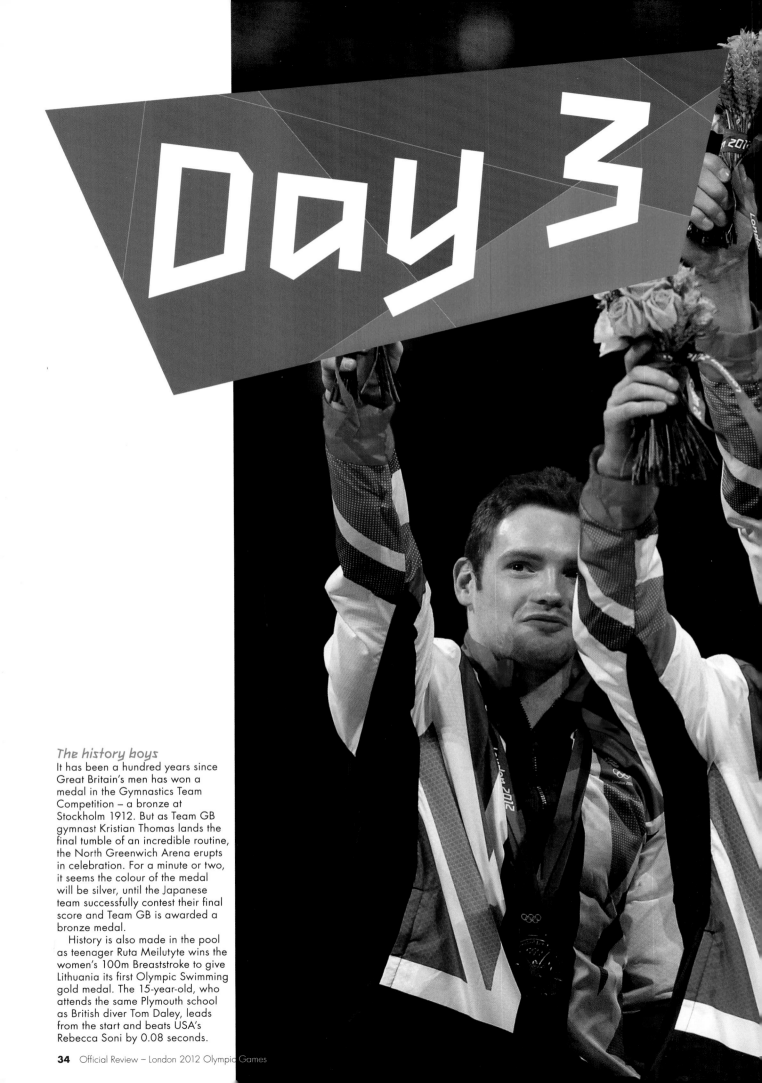

Day 3

The history boys

It has been a hundred years since Great Britain's men has won a medal in the Gymnastics Team Competition – a bronze at Stockholm 1912. But as Team GB gymnast Kristian Thomas lands the final tumble of an incredible routine, the North Greenwich Arena erupts in celebration. For a minute or two, it seems the colour of the medal will be silver, until the Japanese team successfully contest their final score and Team GB is awarded a bronze medal.

History is also made in the pool as teenager Ruta Meilutyte wins the women's 100m Breaststroke to give Lithuania its first Olympic Swimming gold medal. The 15-year-old, who attends the same Plymouth school as British diver Tom Daley, leads from the start and beats USA's Rebecca Soni by 0.08 seconds.

Great Britain's men's gymnasts celebrate winning the country's first medal in the Team Competition in a century

Fencing

The women's Individual Epée gold medal match goes to extra time before Ukraine's **Yana Shemyakina** beats defending champion Britta Heidemann of Germany 9-8 at ExCeL

Rowing

The **Australian** men's Four give the hotly-tipped defending Olympic champions **Great Britain** a scare as they win the qualifying heat in Olympic record time. Both move into the semi-final

Diving

China top the Diving podium for a second day in a row on their quest for a clean sweep of gold medals, as Synchronised 10m Platform pair **Yuan Cao** and **Yanquan Zhang** beat the competition by a comfortable margin

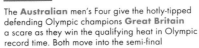

Germany's Peter Thomsen and horse Barny jump the Moon fence in Greenwich Park during the Equestrian – Eventing cross-country round. The obstacle is a reference to the Royal Observatory in the Park

Quote of the day

'Maybe I will visit Buckingham Palace, have tea with The Queen and stroke the corgies'

German fencer Imke Duplitzer sees an upside to an unscheduled day off after losing to Yujie Sun in the women's Individual Epée

Rowing

Great Britain's **Katherine Grainger** and **Anna Watkins** break the Olympic record by four seconds to reach the women's Double Sculls final. Watkins and three-time Olympic silver medallist Grainger are unbeaten in 21 races

Basketball

The long-range shooting of **Evgeniya Belyakova** leads Russian Federation to a 69-59 win over Brazil in the women's Basketball competition

Water Polo

Spain upset China in the opening Group A encounter with an 11-6 victory. Anni Espar scores three goals as Spain turn a 6-4 half-time lead into an unbeatable 10-6 margin at the final break

Katherine Grainger and Anna Watkins get their Olympic gold bid off to a flying start as they qualify for the women's Double Sculls final

★
Star of the day
Ruta Meilutyte

Barry Middleton scores two goals as Great Britain open their men's Hockey account with an eye-catching 4-1 defeat of Argentina at the Riverbank Arena

Born in Lithuania and trained in Plymouth, Ruta Meilutyte wins her country's first gold medal in Swimming in the 100m Breaststroke. Aged only 15, she becomes the youngest gold medal winner in any Swimming event in 16 years. A schoolmate of Great Britain's Tom Daley, Meilutyte's success marks Lithuania's fifth Olympic gold in any sport.

Judo

Russia's **Mansur Isaev** powers to a surprise victory in the men's -73kg Judo event after coming only seventh at the last World Championships

Shooting

Romania's **Alin George Moldoveanu** holds his nerve to take 10m Air Rifle glory ahead of the much-fancied world No.1, Niccolo Camriani of Italy

Swimming

Yannick Agnel of France secures his second gold medal of the Games after victory in the 200m Freestyle – the medal is the 500th gold to be awarded in Swimming at the Olympic Games

Day 3, 30 July

Who won the medals today

Afternoon
Shooting
Men's 10m Air Rifle
- Alin George Moldoveanu (ROU) 702.1
- Niccolo Campriani (ITA) 701.5
- Gagan Narang (IND) 701.1

Afternoon
Diving
Men's Synchronised 10m Platform
- Yuan Cao/Yanquan Zhang (CHN).486.78
- Ivan Garcia Navarro/
  German Sanchez Sanchez (MEX) ..468.90
- David Boudia/
  Nicholas McCrory (USA) 463.47

Afternoon
Judo
Women's -57kg
- Kaori Matsumoto (JPN) 100
- Corina Caprioriu (ROU)................. 000H
- Marti Malloy (USA) 100-0001
- Automne Pavia (FRA) 0011-0002

Afternoon
Judo
Men's -73kg
- Mansur Isaev (RUS) 0011
- Riki Nakaya (JPN)...........................0001
- Nyam-Ochir Sainjargal (MGL) 0011
- Ugo Legrand (FRA).......................... 0101

Afternoon
Weightlifting
Women's 58kg
- Xueying Li (CHN) ....246kg (OR)
- Pimsiri Sirikaew (THA) 236kg
- Yuliya Kalina (UKR) 235kg

Evening
Gymnastics – Artistic
Men's Team
- China 275.997
- Japan 271.952
- Great Britain 271.711

Evening
Swimming
Men's 200m Freestyle
- Yannick Agnel (FRA).................... 1:43.14
- Taehwan Park (KOR) 1:44.93
- Yang Sun (CHN) 1:44.93

Evening
Fencing
Women's Individual Epée
- Yana Shemyakina (UKR) 9
- Britta Heidemann (GER).......................8
- Yujie Sun (CHN) 15-11

Evening
Swimming
Women's 100m Backstroke
- Missy Franklin (USA) 58.33
- Emily Seebohm (AUS).....................58.68
- Aya Terakawa (JPN).......................58.83

Evening
Swimming
Men's 100m Backstroke
- Matthew Grevers (USA)................... 52.16
- Nick Thoman (USA).........................52.92
- Ryosuke Irie (JPN) 52.97

Evening
Weightlifting
Men's 62kg
- Un Guk Kim (PRK) .... 327kg (WR)
- Oscar Albeiro Figueroa
  Mosquera (COL) 317kg
- Irawan Eko Yuli (INA) 317kg

Evening
Swimming
Women's 100m Breaststroke
- Ruta Meilutyte (LTU)................... 1:05.47
- Rebecca Soni (USA) 1:05.55
- Satomi Suzuki (JPN) 1:06.46

Great Britain teenager Zoe Smith smashes the British clean and jerk record en route to finishing 12th in the women's 58kg Weightlifting competition

95%

The percentage of the UK population that were within 10 miles of the Flame during the Torch Relay for the London 2012 Olympic Games

99

The number of training dolls used for Wrestling and Judo during the Games

Zara Phillips, granddaughter of Her Majesty The Queen, enjoys a clear round with no time penalties in the cross-country element in Equestrian Eventing at Greenwich Park

Great Britain's Larry Godfrey progresses through to the last 16 of the Archery men's Individual Competition

1

Yana Shemyakina (UKR) gives Ukraine its first-ever Individual Fencing gold in the women's Individual Epée

Medal table

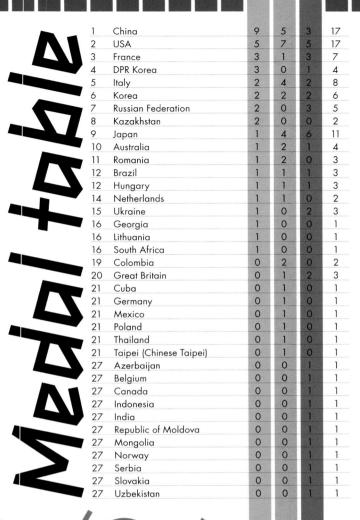

1	China	9	5	3	17
2	USA	5	7	5	17
3	France	3	1	3	7
4	DPR Korea	3	0	1	4
5	Italy	2	4	2	8
6	Korea	2	2	2	6
7	Russian Federation	2	0	3	5
8	Kazakhstan	2	0	0	2
9	Japan	1	4	6	11
10	Australia	1	2	1	4
11	Romania	1	2	0	3
12	Brazil	1	1	1	3
12	Hungary	1	1	1	3
14	Netherlands	1	1	0	2
15	Ukraine	1	0	2	3
16	Georgia	1	0	0	1
16	Lithuania	1	0	0	1
16	South Africa	1	0	0	1
19	Colombia	0	2	0	2
20	Great Britain	0	1	2	3
21	Cuba	0	1	0	1
21	Germany	0	1	0	1
21	Mexico	0	1	0	1
21	Poland	0	1	0	1
21	Thailand	0	1	0	1
21	Taipei (Chinese Taipei)	0	1	0	1
27	Azerbaijan	0	0	1	1
27	Belgium	0	0	1	1
27	Canada	0	0	1	1
27	Indonesia	0	0	1	1
27	India	0	0	1	1
27	Republic of Moldova	0	0	1	1
27	Mongolia	0	0	1	1
27	Norway	0	0	1	1
27	Serbia	0	0	1	1
27	Slovakia	0	0	1	1
27	Uzbekistan	0	0	1	1

20/26

China has now won 20 of the last 26 gold medals in men and women's Diving

American teenager Missy Franklin wins her first Olympic gold in the 100m Backstroke – a feat made even more impressive by the fact she swam in the 200m Freestyle semi-finals only 11 minutes before

36

China become the first nation since Japan, 36 years ago (1960-1976), to win four consecutive gold medals in men's Team Gymnastics

The Duchess of Cambridge and Prince William cheer on cousin Zara Phillips in the Equestrian Eventing competition

Day 4

History is made

As Michael Phelps bows his head on the podium on Day 4 to receive the 15th Olympic gold medal of his phenomenal career, two supporters in the crowd at London's Aquatics Centre wave a banner that reads 'Phelps: Greatest Olympian ever' – a sentiment now confirmed in the history books.

Phelps wins a record 19th Olympic medal as the USA take gold in the 4 x 200m Freestyle Relay making him the most decorated athlete in Olympic Games history.

The gold medal, plus the silver he won an hour earlier in the 200m Butterfly, takes his tally past that of Ukrainian-born gymnast Larissa Latynina, who had held the record for 48 years, with 18 Olympic medals.

Elsewhere, Zara Phillips pays tribute to her team-mates after becoming the first British Royal to win an Olympic medal – a silver in the Eventing Team Competition at Greenwich Park.

Despite failing to defend his Olympic title in the 200m Butterfly moments earlier, USA's Michael Phelps wins his 19th Olympic medal with a gold in the men's 4 x 200m Freestyle Relay

Weightlifting

Kazakhstan wins their third gold of the Games by taking victory in the 63kg division in the women's Weightlifting competition. Maiya Maneza sets an Olympic record, lifting 245kg

Tennis

Great Britain's Andy Murray wins his third round of the men's Tennis competition, brushing aside Finland's Jarkko Nieminen in straight sets at Wimbledon

Hockey

Great Britain maintain their 100 per cent record in the women's Hockey tournament as they edge a Pool A thriller 5-3 against Korea at the Riverbank Arena

Mary King, in a record sixth successive Olympic Games, secures a Team Competition silver medal as part of Great Britain's five-strong Eventing team in front of a passionate 23,000 crowd at Greenwich Park

Quote of the day

'If I had won I would have jumped into the River Thames. Now I do not know what I will do'

Germany's Ole Bischof contemplates his next move after winning silver rather than a gold in the men's Judo -81kg competition

Tony Estanguet continues France's gold medal rush in London by taking top honour in the Canoe Slalom C1 event – it was the Frenchman's third Olympic medal

Judo

Urska Zolnir wins Slovenia's fourth gold medal in Olympic history and their first since Primoz Kozmus in the Hammer Throw in the men's Athletics at Beijing 2008

Football

Steph Houghton scores the winning goal as Team GB defeat Brazil 1-0 in front of a record-breaking crowd of over 70,000 for a women's Football match in the UK

Swimming

South African Swimming sensation Chad le Clos out-touches USA's Michael Phelps at the Aquatics Centre to win the gold medal in the 200m Butterfly final

At just 21-years-old, Egypt's Alaaeldin Abouelkassem claims Africa's first ever medal in Fencing – silver in the men's Individual Foil

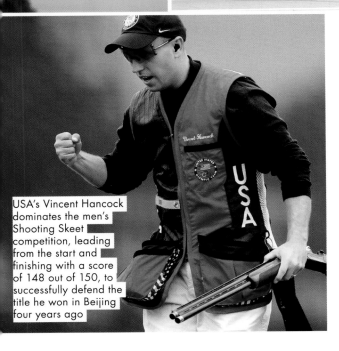

USA's Vincent Hancock dominates the men's Shooting Skeet competition, leading from the start and finishing with a score of 148 out of 150, to successfully defend the title he won in Beijing four years ago

★
Star of the day
Michael Phelps

USA's Michael Phelps becomes the most decorated Olympian in history as he wins his 19th medal – a gold in the Swimming 4 x 200m Freestyle. His 18th medal – a silver in the 400m Individual Medley – could have quite easily been gold, only for the American to be pipped by South Africa's Chad le Clos in the final touch. At 27 years of age, Phelps' 19 medals puts him one ahead of Soviet gymnast Larisa Latynina, who previously held the record for 48 years.

Diving

China adds another Diving gold to their collection as Ruolin Chen and Hao Wang win the women's Synchronised 10m Platform ahead of Mexico (silver) and Canada (bronze)

Swimming

Despite failing to defend his 200m Butterfly title moments earlier, USA's **Michael Phelps** wins his 19th Olympic medal with gold in the 4 x 200m Freestyle Relay, making him the most decorated athlete in Olympic Games history

Swimming

China's **Shiwen Ye** continues her astounding run in the Olympic pool as she wins the 200m Individual Medley, taking the lead in the last 50m after trailing for most of the race

Day 4, 31 July

Who won the medals today

Afternoon
Equestrian
Eventing Team
- Germany...
- Great Britain ....
- New Zealand ....

Afternoon
Shooting
Men's Skeet
- Vincent Hancock (USA) 148
- Anders Golding (DEN) 146
- Nasser Al-Attiya (QAT)...................... 144

Afternoon
Equestrian
Eventing Individual
- Michael Jung (GER)..............................
- Sara Algotsson Ostholt (SWE).................
- Sandra Auffarth (GER)...........................

Afternoon
Canoe Slalom
Men's Canoe Single (C1)
- Tony Estanguet (FRA) 97.06
- Sideris Tasiadis (GER)...................... 98.09
- Michal Martikan (SVK) 98.31

Afternoon
Diving
Women's Synchronised 10m Platform
- Ruolin Chen/Hao Wang (CHN) 368.40
- Paola Espinosa Sanchez/
  Alejandra Orozco Loza (MEX).......343.32
- Meaghan Benfeito/
  Roseline Filion (CAN) 337.62

Afternoon
Judo
Women's -63kg
- Urska Zolnir (RUS) 010
- Lili Xu (CHN) 0011
- Yoshie Ueno (JPN)....................001-0002
- Gevrise Emane (FRA)................. 000-000

Afternoon
Judo
Men's -81kg
- Jae-Bum Kim (KOR) 002
- Ole Bischof (GER) 0001
- Ivan Nifontov (RUS).................0201-000
- Antoine Valois-Fortier (CAN).....0011-000

Afternoon
Weightlifting
Woman's 63kg
- Maiya Maneza (KAZ) ....245kg (OR)
- Svetlana Tsarukaeva (RUS)............. 237kg
- Christine Girard (CAN)................. 236kg

Afternoon
Gymnastics – Artistic
Women's Team
- United States of America 183.596
- Russia 178.530
- Romania 176.414

Evening
Swimming
Women's 200m Freestyle
- Allison Schmitt (USA)............ 1:53.61 (OR)
- Camille Muffat (FRA) 1:55.58
- Bronte Barratt (AUS) 1:55.81

Evening
Fencing
Men's Individual Foil
- Sheng Lei (CHN).......................................
- Alaaeldin Abouelkassem (EGY)...............
- Byungchul Choi (KOR) ....

Evening
Swimming
Men's 200m Butterfly
- Chad le Clos (RSA) 1:52.96
- Michael Phelps (USA) 1:53.01
- Takeshi Matsuda (JPN) 1:53.21

Evening
Weightlifting
Men's 69kg
- Qingfeng Lin (CHN) 344kg
- Triyatno Triyatno (INA) 333kg
- Razvan Constantin Martin (ROU).... 332kg

Evening
Swimming
Women's 200m Individual Medley
- Shiwen Ye (CHN)................. 2:07.57(OR)
- Alicia Coutts (AUS) 2:08.15
- Caitlin Leverenz (USA) 2:08.95

Evening
Swimming
Men's 4 x 200m Freestyle Relay
- USA 6:59.70
- France 7:02.77
- China 7:06.30

USA powers to gold in the women's Artistic Gymnastics, their first Team gold since Atlanta 1996

1996

The last time a non-American swimmer won the 200m Butterfly (Denis Pankratov of Russia), before Chad le Clos (RSA) picks up the gold medal, just ahead of Michael Phelps

48
Number of games needed in the 3rd set for France's Jo-Wilfred Tsonga to overcome Canada's Milos Raonic – it is the longest three-set match in Olympic Games history and takes the total number of games in the match to 66

19
Number of grass courts at Wimbledon, the venue for the London 2012 Tennis tournament

Judo

Korea's Jae-Bum Kim improves on his silver medal from Beijing 2008 to take the gold in the men's Judo -81kg category

Medal table

1	China	13	6	4	23
2	USA	9	8	6	23
3	France	4	3	4	11
4	Korea	3	2	3	8
5	DPR Korea	3	0	1	4
6	Kazakhstan	3	0	0	3
7	Italy	2	4	2	8
8	Germany	2	3	1	6
9	Russian Federation	2	2	4	8
10	South Africa	2	0	0	2
11	Japan	1	4	8	13
12	Australia	1	3	2	6
13	Romania	1	2	2	5
14	Brazil	1	1	1	3
14	Hungary	1	1	1	3
16	Netherlands	1	1	0	2
17	Ukraine	1	0	2	3
18	Georgia	1	0	0	1
18	Lithuania	1	0	0	1
18	Slovenia	1	0	0	1
21	Great Britain	0	2	2	4
22	Colombia	0	2	0	2
22	Mexico	0	2	0	2
24	Indonesia	0	1	1	2
25	Cuba	0	1	0	1
25	Denmark	0	1	0	1
25	Egypt	0	1	0	1
25	Poland	0	1	0	1
25	Sweden	0	1	0	1
25	Taipei (Chinese Taipei)	0	1	0	1
25	Thailand	0	1	0	1
32	Canada	0	0	4	4
33	Slovakia	0	0	2	2
34	Azerbaijan	0	0	1	1
34	Belgium	0	0	1	1
34	India	0	0	1	1
34	Republic of Moldova	0	0	1	1
34	Mongolia	0	0	1	1
34	Norway	0	0	1	1
34	New Zealand	0	0	1	1
34	Qatar	0	0	1	1
34	Serbia	0	0	1	1
34	Uzbekistan	0	0	1	1

70,584

The new UK record for spectators at a women's Football match, reached when Team GB host Brazil at Wembley Stadium, in the last group game of the women's Football competition

Gold rush

Ten days after becoming the first Briton to win the Tour de France, Bradley Wiggins is in action for the second time at London 2012, in the men's Road Cycling Time Trial. With six Olympic medals already to his name, Wiggins has the opportunity to become the most decorated British Olympian of all time, and he doesn't disappoint.

As thousands of spectators line the streets of London's leafy suburbs, Wiggins claims a British record seventh Olympic medal with a sensational gold, stopping the clock at 50:39.54 for the 44km course. Fellow countryman Chris Froome wins the bronze behind Germany's Tony Martin.

Earlier in the day, Great Britain's women's Rowing Pair make history at Eton Dorney. Helen Glover and Heather Stanning dominate the race to win Team GB's first gold medal of London 2012.

Bradley Wiggins sends the home crowd into raptures as he powers to the finish line 42 seconds faster than anyone else in the men's Road Cycling Time Trial to win gold

Day 5

The **German** crew of the men's Eight continue their three-year unbeaten run as they take gold at Eton Dorney ahead of Canada (silver) and Great Britain (bronze)

Xiaoxia Li finally rids herself of the nickname 'Miss No.2' with a comprehensive 4-1 victory over compatriot and world No.1 Ning Ding to take gold in the Table Tennis women's Singles competition

It was Diving gold No.4 in as many days for China as **Yutong Luo** and **Kai Qin** top the podium in the men's Synchronised 3m Springboard

Quote of the day

'I don't remember smiling as I never ever thought "we've got it"'

Helen Glover, who could not contain a straight face in the final 250m of the women's Rowing Pair

Helen Glover (left) and Heather Stanning win Great Britain's first gold of the Games after storming through the final of the women's Pair

Cycling — Road

Kristin Armstrong of USA retains her women's Road Cycling Time Trial title on the streets of Surrey, defeating Germany's Judith Arndt by more than 15 seconds

Weightlifting

Jong Sim Rim wins the women's 69kg Weightlifting, giving DPR Korea four gold medals at the Games and equalling their record medal haul from Barcelona 1992

Archery

15-year-old Moldovan archer **Dan Olaru** hits five 10s from his 12 arrows to defeat Britain's 1992 Olympic bronze medallist Simon Terry in the men's Individual Competition

Japan's star gymnast Kohei Uchimura puts his bad form in the qualification rounds behind him to dominate the Individual All-Around Competition final, adding Olympic gold to his three World Championship titles

★
Star of the day
Bradley Wiggins

Ten days after his historic Tour de France win, Bradley Wiggins wins the men's Road Cycling Time Trial at Hampton Court Palace. His dominant performance secures Wiggins' fourth Olympic Games gold and seventh medal overall, surpassing Sir Steve Redgrave with a British record haul of Games medals.

Daniele Molmenti becomes the first Italian to win a gold medal in Canoe Slalom in 20 years with victory in the men's Kayak Single (K1). Vavrinec Hradilek takes silver – Czech Republic's first medal of the Games

Ruben Limardo Gascon becomes Venezuela's first Olympic Fencing gold medallist by defeating Bartosz Piasecki of Norway, in the men's Individual Epée

Nathan Adrian (USA) wins the men's 100m Freestyle, snatching the gold medal from world champion James Magnussen (AUS) by just one hundredth of a second

Day 5, 1 August

Who won the medals today

Afternoon
Rowing
Women's Pair
- Helen Glover/
  Heather Stanning (GBR) 7:27.13
- Kate Hornsey/Sarah Tait (AUS) 7:29.86
- Juliette Haigh/
  Rebecca Scown (NZL) 7:30.19

Afternoon
Rowing
Women's Quadruple Sculls
- Ukraine 6:35.93
- Germany...6:38.09
- USA..6:40.63

Afternoon
Rowing
Men's Eight
- Germany 5:48.75
- Canada 5:49.98
- Great Britain 5:51.18

Afternoon
Cycling – Road
Women's Individual Time Trial
- Kristin Armstrong (USA) 37:34.82
- Judith Arndt (GER)..................... 37:50.29
- Olga Zabelinskaya (RUS)...........37:57.35

Afternoon
Diving
Men's Synchronised 3m Springboard
- Yutong Luo/Kai Qin (CHN) 477.00
- Ilya Zakharov/
  Evgeny Kuznetsov (RUS)............... 459.63
- Troy Dumais/Kristian Ipsen (USA) ..446.70

Afternoon
Canoe Slalom
Men's Kayak Single (K1)
- Daniele Molmenti (ITA) 93.43
- Vavrinec Hradilek (CZE) 94.78
- Hannes Aigner (GER) 94.92

Afternoon
Shooting
Women's 25m Pistol
- Jangmi Kim (KOR) 792.4
- Ying Chen (CHN)............................791.4
- Olena Kostevych (UKR)...................788.6

Afternoon
Cycling – Road
Men's Individual Time Trial
- Bradley Wiggins (GBR).............. 50:39.54
- Tony Martin (GER).......................51:21.54
- Christopher Froome (GBR) 51:47.87

Afternoon
Judo
Women's -70kg
- Lucie Décosse (FRA) 012
- Kerstin Thiele (GER) 000
- Yuri Alvear (COL)....................011-0001
- Edith Bosch (NED)..................0011-0011

Afternoon
Table Tennis
Women's Singles
- Xiaoxia Li (CHN)................................4
- Ning Ding (CHN)...............................1
- Tianwei Feng (SIN)...........................4-0

Afternoon
Judo
Men's -90kg
- Dae-Nam Song (KOR) 0101
- Asley Gonzalez (CUB)....................0001
- Ilias Iliadis (GRE).................. 0011-0002
- Masashi Nishiyama (JPN)........ 000-0001

Afternoon
Weightlifting
Woman's 69kg
- Jong Sim Rim (PRK).........................261kg
- Roxana Daniela Cocos (ROU) 256kg
- Maryna Shkermankova (BLR)..........256kg

Evening
Gymnastics – Artistic
Men's Individual All-Around
- Kohei Uchimura (JPN)...................92.690
- Marcel Nguyen (GER) 91.031
- Danell Leyva (USA) 90.698

Evening
Swimming
Men's 200m Breaststroke
- Daniel Gyurta (HUN) .... 2:07.28 (WR)
- Michael Jamieson (GBR)............. 2:07.43
- Ryo Tateishi (JPN) 2:08.29

Evening
Swimming
Women's 200m Butterfly
- Liuyang Jiao (CHN)............. 2:04.06 (OR)
- Mireia Belmonte Garcia (ESP) 2:05.25
- Natsumi Hoshi (JPN) 2:05.48

Evening
Weightlifting
Men's 77kg
- Xiaojun Lu (CHN).................. 379kg (WR)
- Haojie Lu (CHN) 360kg
- Ivan Cambar Rodriguez (CUB) 349kg

Evening
Fencing
Men's Individual Epée
- Ruben Limardo Gascon (VEN) 15
- Bartosz Piasecki (NOR) 10
- Jinsun Jung (KOR)........................... 12-11

Evening
Fencing
Women's Individual Sabre
- Jiyeon Kim (KOR) 15
- Sofya Velikaya (RUS)............................9
- Olga Kharlan (UKR) 15-10

Evening
Swimming
Men's 100m Freestyle
- Nathan Adrian (USA) 47.52
- James Magnussen (AUS)................. 47.53
- Brent Hayden (CAN) 47.80

Evening
Swimming
Women's 4 x 200m Freestyle
- USA....................................7:42.92 (OR)
- Australia 7:44.41
- France 7:47.49

42 The winning margin in seconds that Bradley Wiggins enjoys in the 44km Road Cycling Time Trial to claim gold

2.5km TV coverage of Rowing and Canoe Sprint is revolutionised at London 2012 with the world's longest cable camera. Suspended on three wires and stretched at each end of the 2.5km lake at Eton Dorney, it gives television viewers a completely different angle

London's iconic Tower Bridge shines gold in celebration of Great Britain's gold medal success on Day 5

Wimbledon finalist **Andy Murray** beats Marcos Baghdatis of Cyprus to reach the Tennis men's Singles quarter-finals

Great Britain's men's Eight win a bronze medal in a nail-biting final at Eton Dorney. It is the third Olympic medal for 40-year-old Greg Searle

Michael Jamieson puts in an outstanding performance to become the first British man to claim a medal at the Aquatics Centre – silver in the 200m Breaststroke

Medal table

1	China	17	9	4	30
2	USA	12	8	9	29
3	Korea	6	2	4	12
4	France	5	3	5	13
5	DPR Korea	4	0	1	5
6	Germany	3	8	2	13
7	Italy	3	4	2	9
8	Kazakhstan	3	0	0	3
9	Japan	2	4	11	17
10	Russian Federation	2	4	5	11
11	Great Britain	2	3	4	9
12	Hungary	2	1	1	4
13	Ukraine	2	0	4	6
14	South Africa	2	0	0	2
15	Australia	1	6	2	9
16	Romania	1	3	2	6
17	Brazil	1	1	1	3
17	Netherlands	1	1	1	3
19	Georgia	1	0	0	1
19	Lithuania	1	0	0	1
19	Slovenia	1	0	0	1
19	Venezuela	1	0	0	1
23	Colombia	0	2	1	3
23	Cuba	0	2	1	3
25	Mexico	0	2	0	2
26	Canada	0	1	5	6
27	Indonesia	0	1	1	2
27	Norway	0	1	1	2
29	Czech Republic	0	1	0	1
29	Denmark	0	1	0	1
29	Egypt	0	1	0	1
29	Poland	0	1	0	1
29	Spain	0	1	0	1
29	Sweden	0	1	0	1
29	Taipei (Chinese Taipei)	0	1	0	1
29	Thailand	0	1	0	1
37	New Zealand	0	0	2	2
37	Slovakia	0	0	2	2
39	Azerbaijan	0	0	1	1
39	Belarus	0	0	1	1
39	Belgium	0	0	1	1
39	Greece	0	0	1	1
39	India	0	0	1	1
39	Republic of Moldova	0	0	1	1
39	Mongolia	0	0	1	1
39	Qatar	0	0	1	1
39	Serbia	0	0	1	1
39	Singapore	0	0	1	1
39	Uzbekistan	0	0	1	1

12,000
The wave shaped roof on the London 2012 Aquatics Centre measures 12,000 square metres, which is one and a half times bigger than Wembley's football pitch

Great Britain top their group in the men's Football competition and advance to the quarter-finals. A Daniel Sturridge strike earns them a 1-0 victory against Uruguay in Cardiff

1/100th
In the men's 100m Freestyle final, Nathan Adrian beats James Magnussen by one hundredth of a second – the smallest winning margin in this event since they started measuring time in one hundredths of a second after Munich 1972

Tim Baillie (left) and Etienne Stott of Great Britain power their way to the gold medal in the men's Canoe Double (C2) at Lee Valley White Water Centre

Day 6

Riding the wave

The Host Nation enjoys its best day of the London 2012 Games so far, but Britain is not the only one celebrating on a dramatic Day 6. Sir Chris Hoy hails his fifth Olympic gold as his best ever, after Great Britain's men's Team Sprint squad triumph on a night of high drama at the Velodrome.

Elsewhere, Britain claims two gold medals in the space of five minutes. First, Etienne Stott and Tim Baillie lead a British one-two in the Canoe Double (C2), with David Florence and Richard Hounslow finishing second. And in a joyful show of Olympic spirit, all four British athletes, with their coaches, jump into the water and celebrate together as one team.

It's also a memorable night for USA in the pool, with Michael Phelps leading the way. He claims his 20th Olympic medal and his first individual gold of London 2012 in the 200m Individual Medley.

In a nail-biting final at Eton Dorney, **Great Britain's** Lightweight men's Four take silver behind South Africa by a mere quarter of a second, with defending champions Denmark picking up bronze

USA's **Gabrielle Douglas** adds Individual All-Around gold to her Team gold, edging out Russia's Victoria Komova and Aliya Mustafina who take silver and bronze respectively

Michael Phelps beats his rival and team-mate Ryan Lochte in the much-anticipated men's 200m Individual Medley final. The gold brings Phelps' Olympic medal haul to 20

Quote of the day

'It doesn't really seem real yet, but it's amazing. Of course it's amazing. The crowd was amazing. I wish it could be gold for them but it wasn't to be'

Gemma Gibbons on her silver medal in the Judo women's -78kg

Cycling — Track

Great Britain post a world record time in qualification for the men's Team Pursuit. Ed Clancy, Steven Burke, Peter Kennaugh and Geraint Thomas clock 3:52.499 for the 4000m distance

Hockey

Great Britain preserve their 100 per cent Pool A record in the women's Hockey tournament with a 3-0 defeat of Belgium at the Riverbank Arena

Boxing

British Middle Weight **Anthony Ogogo** defeats world No.1 Ievgen Khytrov of Ukraine on the judges' verdict. After three brutal rounds the bout ended 18-18 at ExCeL

After a run of first and second round exits by British judoka, GBR's Gemma Gibbons (left) defeats -78kg French world champion Audrey Tcheumeo on her way to the final, where she secures a silver medal

Coached by a Dubai prince, Britain's Peter Wilson shoots his way to gold in the Double Trap. In doing so, he emulates his team-mate Richard Faulds' feat at Sydney 2000

★
Star of the day
Peter Wilson

A farmer's son from Dorset, Peter Robert Russell Wilson becomes a household name as he notches up Britain's fourth gold of London 2012, in the Shooting Double Trap competition, at The Royal Artillery Barracks. Wilson came into the event as a world record holder and world No.2, and was the youngest man in the final. It is Britain's first Olympic shooting medal since Richard Faulds – who failed to reach the six-man final this time – won gold in the same event at Sydney 2000.

Victoria Pendleton is left frustrated after she and Jess Varnish are disqualified from the women's Team Sprint after an illegal changeover in the first round against Ukraine. They had earlier set a world record in qualification

Following their clean sweep of medals in the Individual Foil, **Italy's** women claim the Team gold with a 45-31 victory over defending champions Russia

USA's **Rebecca Soni** breaks the 200m Breaststroke world record for a second time in as many days, becoming the first woman to dip under 2min 20sec to take gold

Day 6, 2 August

Who won the medals today

Afternoon
Rowing
Men's Double Sculls
- Nathan Cohen/ Joseph Sullivan (NZ)................... 6:31.67
- Alessio Sartori/ Romano Battisti (ITA)................. 6:32.80
- Luka Spik/Iztok Cop (SVK)........... 6:34.35

Afternoon
Rowing
Lightweight men's Four
- South Africa 6:02.84
- Great Britain 6:03.09
- Denmark 6:03.16

Afternoon
Rowing
Women's Eight
- USA... 6:10.59
- Canada 6:12.06
- Netherlands 6:13.12

Afternoon
Shooting
Men's Double Trap
- Peter Wilson (GBR)........................... 188
- Hakan Dahlby (SWE) 186
- Vasily Mosin (RUS) 185

Afternoon
Archery
Women's Individual
- Bo Bae Ki (KOR) 6
- Aida Roman (ITA) 5
- Mariana Avitia (MEX) 6-2

Afternoon
Judo
Women's -78 kg
- Kayla Harrison (USA) 002
- Gemma Gibbons (GBR) 000
- Audrey Tcheumeo (FRA)........... 100-0001
- Mayra Aguiar (BRA)................. 100-000

Afternoon
Canoe Slalom
Men's Canoe Double (C2)
- Tim Baillie/Etienne Stott (GBR)....... 106.41
- David Florence/ Richard Hounslow (GBR)...............106.77
- Pavol Hochschorner/ Peter Hochschorner (SVK) 108.28

Afternoon
Judo
Men's -100kg
- Tagir Khaibulaev (RUS) 100
- Tuvshinbayar Naidan (MGL) 000
- Dimitri Peters (GER) 020-001
- Henk Grol (NED) 010-000

Afternoon
Table Tennis
Men's Singles
- Jike Zhang (CHN) 4
- Hao Wang (CHN) 1
- Dimitrij Ovtcharov (GER)...................4-2

Afternoon
Canoe Slalom
Women's Kayak Single (K1)
- Emilie Fer (FRA)........................... 105.90
- Jessica Fox (AUS) 106.51
- Maialen Chourraut (ESP)............... 106.87

Afternoon
Cycling – Track
Women's Team Sprint
- Germany....................................32.798
- China .... Relegated
- Australia 32.727

Afternoon
Cycling – Track
Men's Team Sprint
- Great Britain .... 42.600 (WR)
- France 43.013
- Germany....................................43.209

Afternoon
Gymnastics – Artistic
Women's Individual All-Around
- Gabrielle Douglas (USA) 62.232
- Victoria Komova (RUS) 61.973
- Aliya Mustafina (RUS)................. 59.566

Evening
Swimming
Women's 200m Breaststroke
- Rebecca Soni (USA) .... 2:19.59 (WR)
- Satomi Suzuki (JPN) 2:20.72
- Iuliia Efimova (RUS) 2:20.92

Evening
Swimming
Men's 200m Backstroke
- Tyler Clary (USA) ....1:53.41 (OR)
- Ryosuke Irie (JPN) 1:53.78
- Ryan Lochte (USA).......................1:53.94

Evening
Swimming
Men's 200m Individual Medley
- Michael Phelps (USA) 1:54.27
- Ryan Lochte (USA)......................1:54.90
- Laszlo Cseh (HUN).....................1:56.22

Evening
Fencing
Women's Team Foil
- Italy..45
- Russian Federation 31
- Korea 45-32

Evening
Swimming
Women's 100m Freestyle
- Ranomi Kromowidjojo (NED)... 53.00 (OR)
- Aliaksandra Herasimenia (BLR)........53.38
- Yi Tang (CHN) 53.44

24 Number of years since Great Britain have won gold and silver in the same event, until Tim Baillie with Etienne Stott and David Florence with Richard Hounslow win gold and silver, respectively, in the Canoe Slalom men's Canoe Double (C2)

4 Anna Meares (Australia) becomes the first woman to win four Olympic medals in Track Cycling

52 years, 317 days Age of silver medallist Lesley Thompson-Willie of Canada; their win in the Rowing women's Eight made her Canada's record Rowing medallist, with five. She is also the second oldest Olympic medal winner in Rowing

Hiroshi Hoketsu (JPN), riding Whisper, is the oldest competitor taking part at London 2012 – aged 71

Sir Chris Hoy (right), with the help of Philip Hindes (left) and Jason Kenny, lands a fifth Olympic gold medal as Great Britain win the Track Cycling men's Team Sprint, in a world record time of 42.600

Table tennis

Jike Zhang of China completes a grand slam, adding Olympic gold to his World Championship and World Cup titles following his 4-1 win over compatriot Hao Wang

Basketball

Team GB lose out by just one point in a thrilling Group B preliminary round game against Spain with a final score of 79-78

Medal table

1	China	18	11	5	34
2	USA	18	9	10	37
3	Korea	7	2	5	14
4	France	6	4	6	16
5	Great Britain	5	6	4	15
6	Germany	4	8	5	17
7	Italy	4	5	2	11
8	DPR Korea	4	0	1	5
9	Russian Federation	3	6	8	17
10	Kazakhstan	3	0	0	3
10	South Africa	3	0	0	3
12	Japan	2	6	11	19
13	Netherlands	2	1	3	6
14	Hungary	2	1	2	5
15	Ukraine	2	0	4	6
16	Australia	1	7	3	11
17	Romania	1	3	2	6
18	Brazil	1	1	2	4
19	New Zealand	1	0	2	3
20	Slovenia	1	0	1	2
21	Georgia	1	0	0	1
21	Lithuania	1	0	0	1
21	Venezuela	1	0	0	1
24	Mexico	0	3	1	4
25	Canada	0	2	5	7
26	Colombia	0	2	1	3
26	Cuba	0	2	1	3
28	Sweden	0	2	0	2
29	Belarus	0	1	1	2
29	Denmark	0	1	1	2
29	Indonesia	0	1	1	2
29	Mongolia	0	1	1	2
29	Norway	0	1	1	2
29	Spain	0	1	1	2
35	Czech Republic	0	1	0	1
35	Egypt	0	1	0	1
35	Poland	0	1	0	1
35	Taipei (Chinese Taipei)	0	1	0	1
35	Thailand	0	1	0	1
40	Slovakia	0	0	3	3
41	Azerbaijan	0	0	1	1
41	Belgium	0	0	1	1
41	Greece	0	0	1	1
41	India	0	0	1	1
41	Republic of Moldova	0	0	1	1
41	Qatar	0	0	1	1
41	Serbia	0	0	1	1
41	Singapore	0	0	1	1
41	Uzbekistan	0	0	1	1

6

Valentina Vezzali becomes the first woman to win six gold medals in Fencing, after Italy wins gold in the Team Foil Competition

To the amazement of commuters, Venezuela's first Olympic Fencing gold medallist, Ruben Limardo Gascon, travels on the London Underground wearing his Fencing Individual Epée medal

Day 7

After three successive
silver medals in as
many Olympic Games,
Team GB's Katherine
Grainger, along with
Rowing partner Anna
Watkins, grab
gold in a thrilling
Double Sculls final

The eagerly awaited Athletics events finally get under way at the Olympic Stadium, with Great Britain's poster girl Jessica Ennis starting her bid for glory in the Heptathlon.

Ennis begins her account in the morning in two of her favoured events – the 100m hurdles and the high jump. She gets off to the perfect start, destroying her personal best in the 100m hurdles by 0.25sec, in the fastest ever time set by a heptathlete in the event.

At Eton Dorney, rowers Katherine Grainger and Anna Watkins win Great Britain's first gold medal of the day, in the women's Double Sculls. The victory means Grainger finally earns gold after winning silver at the three previous Olympic Games.

Capping off a sensational evening for Britain's track cyclists at the Velodrome, Victoria Pendleton sprints to victory in the women's Keirin. Half an hour earlier, Team GB's men's Team Pursuit squad claim a thrilling Olympic gold in a world record time of 3:51.659, to successfully defend the title Britain won at Beijing 2008.

Weightlifting

Kazakhstan's **Svetlana Podobedova** smashes the Olympic record to win gold in the women's 75kg Weightlifting competition with a lift of 291kg

Cycling — Track

Great Britain's trio of **Joanna Rowsell, Dani King and Laura Trott** break the world record in the women's Team Pursuit, recording a time of 3:15.669 in qualification

Equestrian — Dressage

Charlotte Dujardin sets a new Olympic record with a score of 83.66 per cent to put her top of the Individual Dressage rankings

Jessica Ennis runs the fastest 100m hurdles in a Heptathlon to help the Briton to her best ever first-day score of 4158pts. Overnight, she holds a 184pt advantage over her nearest rival, Austra Skujyte of Lithuania

Quote of the day

'I am not disappointed to get a bronze medal. I gave it my all and I'm proud to be on the podium'

Rebecca Adlington on winning bronze in the women's 800m Freestyle final

Rebecca Adlington congratulates 15-year-old Katie Ledecky of the USA after their 800m Freestyle final – Adlington finishes third to take her second bronze of the Games

Mahe Drysdale of New Zealand improves on his bronze medal from Beijing 2008 to win gold in the men's Single Sculls final at Eton Dorney, stopping the clock in 6:57.82

Great Britain retain their men's Team Pursuit title from Beijing 2008 – overcoming Australia to clinch gold in a new world record of 3:51.659

Missy Franklin adds to an incredible night in the pool for USA as she wins gold in the women's 200m Backstroke in a world record time of 2:04.06

Victoria Pendleton (centre) bounces back just 24 hours after disqualification from the Team Sprint to win the women's Keirin in style

Roger Federer and Juan Martin del Potro make history in their Tennis Singles semi-final by playing the longest three-set men's singles match in the Open era – 4 hours and 23 minutes

★
Star of the day
Tirunesh Dibaba

The Ethiopian runner takes the first gold medal in the Athletics programme as she defends her women's 10,000m title from Beijing 2008, in 30:20.75. The gold medal equals the feat of her cousin Derartu Tulu, who won at Barcelona 1992 and Sydney 2000, as the only woman to win two gold medals in the event since it was introduced at the Olympic Games at Seoul 1988.

Karina Bryant wins bronze in the women's Judo +78kg. It's the second Judo medal for GBR's women after the silver won by Gemma Gibbons in the -78kg category

Errol Spence is the only USA boxer left in the Boxing competition after winning an appeal to have the result of his bout with India's Krishan Vikas reversed

Leuris Pupo outshoots Russian favourite Alexei Klimov to claim Cuba's first gold of the London Games – in the 25m Rapid Fire Pistol event

Day 7, 3 August

Who won the medals today

Afternoon
Rowing
Men's Quadruple Sculls
- Germany 5:42.48
- Croatia 5:44.78
- Australia 5:45.22

Afternoon
Rowing
Men's Pair
- Eric Murray/Hamish Bond (NZL)... 6:16.65
- Germain Chardin/
  Dorian Mortelette (FRA)................6:21.11
- George Nash/
  William Satch (GBR) 6:21.77

Afternoon
Shooting
Men's 50m Rifle Prone
- Sergei Martynov (BLR) 705.5
- Lionel Cox (BEL) 701.2
- Rajmond Debevec (SLO) 701.0

Afternoon
Rowing
Women's Double Sculls
- Anna Watkings/
  Katherine Grainger (GBR) 6:55.82
- Kim Crow/Brooke Pratley (AUS) ...6:58.55
- Magdalena Fularczyk/
  Julia Michalska (POL) 7:07.92

Afternoon
Rowing
Men's Single Sculls
- Mahe Drysdale (NZL) 6:57.82
- Ondrej Synek (CZE) 6:59.37
- Alan Campbell (GBR) 7:03.28

Afternoon
Shooting
Men's 25m Rapid Fire Pistol
- Leuris Pupo (CUB) 34
- Vijay Kumar (IND) 30
- Feng Ding (CHN) 27

Afternoon
Archery
Men's Individual
- Jin Hyek Oh (KOR) 7
- Takaharu Furukawa (JPN) 1
- Xiaoxiang Dai (CHN) 6-5

Afternoon
Gymnastics – Trampoline
Men
- Dong Dong (CHN) 62.990
- Dmitry Ushakov (RUS) 61.769
- Chunlong Lu (CHN) 61.319

Afternoon
Judo
Women's +78 kg
- Idalys Ortiz (CUB)............................ 000
- Mika Sugimoto (JPN) 0001
- Karina Bryant (GBR) 020-011
- Wen Tong (CHN) 100-0001

Afternoon
Judo
Men's +100kg
- Teddy Riner (FRA) 0101
- Alexander Mikhaylin (RUS) 0003
- Andreas Toelzer (GER) 100
- Rafael Silva (BRA) 0011-0002

Afternoon
Badminton
Mixed Doubles
- Nan Zhang/Yunlei Zhao (CHN) 21, 21
- Chen Xu/
  Jin Ma (CHN)...............................11, 17
- Joachim Fischer/
  Christinna Pedersen (DEN) 21-12, 21-12

Afternoon
Weightlifting
Women's 75kg
- Svetlana Podobedova (KAZ) 291
- Natalya Zabolotnaya (RUS) 291
- Iryna Kulesha (BLR) 269

Afternoon
Cycling – Track
Men's Team Pursuit
- Great Britain 3:51.659
- Australia 3:54.581
- New Zealand 3:55.952

Afternoon
Cycling – Track
Women's Keirin
- Victoria Pendleton (GBR)...............10.965
- Shuang Guo (CHN) ....n/a
- Wai Sze Lee (HKG) ....n/a

Evening
Fencing
Men's Team Sabre
- Korea 45
- Romania 26
- Italy...45-40

Evening
Athletics
Men's Shot Put
- Tomasz Majewski (POL) 21.89
- David Storl (GER) 21.86
- Reese Hoffa (USA) 21.23

Evening
Weightlifting
Men's 85kg
- Adrian Edward Zielinski (POL)............385
- Apti Aukhadov (RUS).........................385
- Kianoush Rostami (IRI) 380

Evening
Athletics
Women's 10,000m
- Tirunesh Dibaba (ETH).............30:20.75
- Sally Jepkosgei Kipyego (KEN)...30:26.37
- Vivian Jepkemoi Cheruiyot (KEN).30:30.44

Evening
Swimming
Women's 200m Backstroke
- Missy Franklin (USA) 2:04.06
- Anastasia Zueva (RUS) 2:05.92
- Elizabeth Beisel (USA) 2:06.55

Evening
Swimming
Men's 100m Butterfly
- Michael Phelps (USA) 51.21
- Chad Le Clos (RSA) 51.44
- Evgeny Korotyshkin (RUS) 51.44

Evening
Swimming
Women's 800m Freestyle
- Katie Ledecky (USA) 8:14.63
- Mireia Belmonte Garcia (ESP) 8:18.76
- Rebecca Adlington (GBR) 8:20.32

Evening
Swimming
Men's 50m Freestyle
- Florent Manaudou (FRA) 21.34
- Cullen Jones (USA) 21.54
- Cesar Cielo (BRA) 21.59

Ashley Jackson scores twice as Great Britain beat Pakistan 4-1 to put their hopes of reaching the Hockey semi-finals back on track after a disappointing draw against South Africa

36

China becomes the first National Olympic Committee since Japan, 36 years ago (1960-76), to win four consecutive golds in men's Team Artistic Gymnastics

Florent Manaudou emerges as the surprise winner of the men's 50m Freestyle to take France's gold medal haul at the Aquatics Centre to four – double their previous best

Fencing

Korea prove the surprise package of the men's Team Sabre event, pulling off a 45-26 win over Romania to take gold

Swimming

Michael Phelps wins his third gold of the Games – and his 21st medal overall – as he defends his 100m Butterfly title in his final individual swim

Ben Ainslie has a fourth Olympic gold medal in his sights after his tactical sailing forced his Danish rival Jonas Høgh-Christensen into third place in race 10 of the Finn class

Medal table

1	USA	21	10	12	43
2	China	20	13	9	42
3	Korea	9	2	5	16
4	Great Britain	8	6	8	22
5	France	8	5	6	19
6	Germany	5	9	6	20
7	Italy	4	5	3	12
8	DPR Korea	4	0	1	5
9	Kazakhstan	4	0	0	4
10	Russian Federation	3	12	8	23
11	South Africa	3	1	0	4
12	New Zealand	3	0	3	6
13	Japan	2	8	11	21
14	Cuba	2	2	1	5
15	Netherlands	2	1	3	6
16	Hungary	2	1	2	5
17	Poland	2	1	1	4
18	Ukraine	2	0	4	6
19	Australia	1	9	4	14
20	Romania	1	4	2	7
21	Brazil	1	1	4	6
22	Belarus	1	1	2	4
23	Slovenia	1	0	2	3
24	Ethiopia	1	0	0	1
24	Georgia	1	0	0	1
24	Lithuania	1	0	0	1
24	Venezuela	1	0	0	1
28	Mexico	0	3	1	4
29	Canada	0	2	5	7
30	Colombia	0	2	1	3
30	Spain	0	2	1	3
32	Czech Republic	0	2	0	2
32	Sweden	0	2	0	2
34	Denmark	0	1	2	3
35	Belgium	0	1	1	2
35	Indonesia	0	1	1	2
35	India	0	1	1	2
35	Kenya	0	1	1	2
35	Mongolia	0	1	1	2
35	Norway	0	1	1	2
41	Croatia	0	1	0	1
41	Egypt	0	1	0	1
41	Thailand	0	1	0	1
41	Taipei (Chinese Taipei)	0	1	0	1
45	Slovakia	0	0	3	3
46	Azerbaijan	0	0	1	1
46	Greece	0	0	1	1
46	Hong Kong	0	0	1	1
46	Iran	0	0	1	1
46	Republic of Moldova	0	0	1	1
46	Qatar	0	0	1	1
46	Singapore	0	0	1	1
46	Serbia	0	0	1	1
46	Uzbekistan	0	0	1	1

Runners pass by the Olympic Flame on the first day of Athletics in the Olympic Stadium at London 2012

600

The number of workers required to dismantle the set of the Opening Ceremony in time for the Athletics events to get under way at the Olympic Stadium

Hosts make history

It's a day like no other, the day that Great Britain delivers its best single-day performance in 104 years of Olympic competition.

In front of a roaring, 80,000-strong crowd at the Olympic Stadium, Jessica Ennis holds firm in the long jump and javelin before winning her 800m heat to secure the Heptathlon gold medal. Having wiped away the misery of missing out through injury at Beijing 2008, the Briton becomes the first woman to win the Olympic Heptathlon on home soil.

Later in the evening, Greg Rutherford's 8.31m in the Long Jump gives Great Britain its first gold medal in this men's event since Lynn Davies achieved the same feat at Tokyo 1964.

Mo Farah then becomes the first athlete not representing an African National Olympic Committee to win the 10,000m since Italy's Alberto Cova in 1984. Farah's last lap is a blistering 53 seconds, as he takes gold ahead of training partner, Galen Rupp of the USA.

In the Velodrome, Joanna Rowsell, Dani King and Laura Trott romp home in the women's Team Pursuit against Canada, winning the gold medal in a world record time of 3:14.682.

Meanwhile, on the final day of Rowing at Eton Dorney, Great Britain continue to dominate the regatta as Andrew Triggs Hodge, Pete Reed, Tom James and Steve Williams row to victory in the men's Four. Katherine Copeland and Sophie Hosking also secure gold in the Lightweight women's Double Sculls, before Zac Purchase and Mark Hunter take silver in the Lightweight men's Double Sculls.

Britain's greatest Olympic day for over 104 years!

Jessica Ennis jumps 6.48m in the long jump en route to victory in the Heptathlon

Swimming

USA's women complete their dominance in the pool with a world record in the 4 x 100m Medley Relay. Australia and Japan take silver and bronze respectively

Tennis

Serena Williams of USA becomes the first woman to claim the Tennis 'Golden Slam' in both Singles and Doubles after she defeats Russia's Maria Sharapova 6-0 6-1

Rowing

After a delay to the race caused by equipment failure, Britons **Mark Hunter and Zac Purchase** are pipped to gold in the men's Lightweight Double Scull by Danes Mads Rasmussen and Rasmus Quist

Greg Rutherford springs the surprise of the night, leaping 8.31m to take Long Jump gold ahead of Mitchell Watt of Australia (8.16m) and USA's Will Claye (8.12m)

Mo Farah makes it a British treble, bringing an end to a phenomenal evening for the Host Nation with victory in the men's 10,000m. In doing so, Farah, who is also to compete in the 5000m at London 2012, becomes the first British winner of the event

Quote of the day

'I'm definitely going to relax, eat lots of rubbish food, have a few glasses of wine and enjoy this moment for as long as possible'

Jessica Ennis plans on taking it easy after winning gold in the Heptathlon

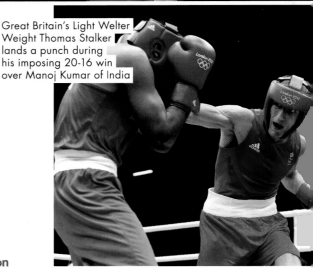

Great Britain's Light Welter Weight Thomas Stalker lands a punch during his imposing 20-16 win over Manoj Kumar of India

Badminton

China's **Yunlei Zhao** makes Olympic Badminton history when she becomes the first player to win two golds at the same Games, following up her Mixed Doubles success with victory in the women's Doubles

Triathlon

Nicola Spirig of Switzerland charges through Hyde Park on her way to a thrilling photo-finish victory over Sweden's Lisa Norden in the women's Triathlon

Swimming

The most decorated Olympian in the world, **Michael Phelps** finishes his swimming career on a high as he picks up his 18th Olympic gold after leading USA to glory in the 4 x 100m Medley Relay

China's Yang Sun powers his way to 1500m Freestyle gold in world record time, sparking wild celebrations. This is his second gold of the Games, after topping the podium in the 400m Freestyle in Olympic record time, adding to his silver (200m Freestyle) and bronze (4 x 200m Freestyle Relay)

Great Britain's crew of Andrew Triggs Hodge, Pete Reed, Tom James and Alex Gregory row to Olympic gold in the final of the men's Four, maintaining Britain's reputation in the event with a fourth consecutive Olympic title

★
Star of the day
Jessica Ennis

As the poster girl of London 2012, it is almost scripted that Jessica Ennis will win Great Britain's first gold of the Athletics programme. With an 188-point lead in the Heptathlon after six events, Ennis goes into the 800m needing to finish within eight seconds of her nearest rival, Austra Skujyte of Lithuania. But Ennis finishes off the competition in style, fighting back in the home straight to clock a time of 2:08.65 – breaking the British Heptathlon record for the second time this year as she takes the gold.

Gymnastics – Trampoline

Gymnast **Rosannagh MacLennan** brings Canada their first gold medal of the Games by winning the women's Individual Trampoline final, beating defending champion Wenna He of China

Swimming

Ranomi Kromowidjojo of the Netherlands completes a sprint double by adding 50m Freestyle gold to the 100m Freestyle title she claimed earlier in the week

Athletics

Shelly-Ann Fraser-Pryce of Jamaica defends her 100m title, edging out world champion Carmelita Jeter of USA by 0.03sec, to win in a time of 10.75

Day 8, 4 August

Who won the medals today

Morning
Triathlon
Women
- Nicola Spirig (SUI).....................1:59:48
- Lisa Norden (SWE) 1:59:48
- Erin Densham (AUS 1:59:50

Afternoon
Rowing
Men's Four
- Great Britain 6:03.97
- Australia 6:05:19
- USA...6:07:20

Afternoon
Rowing
Lightweight women's Double Sculls
- Great Britain 7:09:30
- China 7:11.93
- Greece 7:12.09

Afternoon
Rowing
Lightweight men's Double Sculls
- Denmark 6:37.17
- Great Britain 6:37.78
- New Zealand 6:40.86

Afternoon
Rowing
Women's Single Sculls
- Miroslava Knapkova (CZE) 7:54.37
- Fie Udby Erichsen (DEN)..............7:57.72
- Kim Crow (AUS) 7:58.04

Afternoon
Shooting
Women's 50m Rifle 3 Position
- Jamie Lynn Gray (USA) 691.9
- Ivana Maksimovic (SRB) 687.5
- Adela Sykorova (CZE) 683.0

Afternoon
Badminton
Women's Singles
- Xuerui Li (CHN)..............21, 21, 21
- Yihan Wang (CHN) 15, 23, 17
- Saina Nehwal (IND)......(opponent retired)

Afternoon
Tennis
Women's Singles
- Serena Williams (USA) 6, 6
- Maria Sharapova (RUS)....................0, 1
- Victoria Azarenka (BLR) 6-3, 6-4

Afternoon
Shooting
Women's Trap
- Jessica Rossi (ITA)................................99
- Zuzana Stefecekova (SVK) 93
- Delphine Reau (FRA) 93

Afternoon
Gymnastics – Trampoline
Women
- Rosannagh Maclennan (CAN) 57.305
- Shanshan Huang (CHN)..............56.730
- Wenna He (CHN) 55.950

Afternoon
Badminton
Women's Doubles
- Yunlei Zhao & Qing Tian (CHN).....21, 25
- Reika Kakiiwa & Mizuki Fujii (JPN).. 10, 23
- V Sorokina & N Vislova (RUS) ..21-9, 21-10

Afternoon
Tennis
Men's Doubles
- Mike Bryan & Bob Bryan (USA)..........6, 7
- Michael Llodra & Jo-W Tsonga (FRA) ..4, 6
- J Benneteau & R Gasquet (FRA) 7-6, 6-2

Afternoon
Cycling – Track
Women's Team Pursuit
- Great Britain 3:14.051
- USA 3:19.727
- Canada 3:17.915

Afternoon
Athletics
Men's 20k Race Walk
- Ding Chen (CHN) 1:18:46
- Erick Barrondo (GUA) 1:18:57
- Zhen Wang (CHN 1:19:25

Evening
Athletics
Women's Discus Throw
- Sandra Perkovic (CRO).................69.11m
- Darya Pishchalnikova (RUS) 67.56m
- Yanfeng Li (CHN).......................67.22m

Evening
Fencing
Women's Team Epée
- China 39
- Korea 25
- USA.......................................31-30

Evening
Weightlifting
Men's 94kg
- Ilya Ilyin (KAZ) 418
- Alexandr Invanov (RUS) 409
- Anatoli Ciricu (MDA).....................407

Evening
Athletics
Women's Heptathlon
- Jessica Ennis (GBR) 6955
- Lilli Schwarzkopf (GER)....................6649
- Tatyana Chernova (RUS).................6628

Evening
Athletics
Women's Long Jump
- Greg Rutherford (GBR) 8.31m
- Mitchell Watt (AUS) 8.16m
- Will Claye (USA) 8.12m

Evening
Athletics
Men's 10,000m
- Mohammed Farah (GBR) 27:30.42
- Galen Rupp (USA)....................27:30.90
- Tariku Bekele (ETH) 27:31.43

Evening
Athletics
Women's 100m
- Shelly-Ann Fraser-Pryce (JAM)........ 10.75
- Carmelita Jeter (USA) 10.78
- Veronica Campbell-Brown (JAM)..... 10.81

Evening
Swimming
Women's 50m Freestyle
- Ranomi Kromowidjojo (NED)...........24.05
- Aliaksandra Herasimenia (BLR)........24.28
- Marleen Veldhuis (NED) 24.39

Evening
Swimming
Men's 1500m Freestyle
- Yang Sun (CHN) 14:31.02
- Ryan Cochrane (CAN) 14:39.63
- Oussama Mellouli (TUN) 14:40.31

Evening
Swimming
Women's 4 x 100m Medley Relay
- USA.......................................3:52.05
- Australia 3:54.02
- Japan 3:55.73

Evening
Swimming
Men's 4 x 100m Medley Relay
- USA 3:29.35
- Japan 3:31.26
- Australia 3:31.58

20 years 102 days

Briton Laura Trott becomes the youngest gold medallist in women's Track Cycling at the Olympic Games

USA win the men's 4 x 100m Medley Relay for the eighth time in a row – their longest streak in a single Swimming event

The girl with the infectious smile, Katarina Johnson-Thompson, breaks her own British junior record with 6,267 points as she finishes 15th in the Heptathlon

Lightweight women's Double Sculls pair
Sophie Hosking and Katherine Copeland take Britain's fourth Rowing gold by beating China and Greece at Eton Dorney

Medal table

		G	S	B	Total
1	USA	26	13	15	54
2	China	25	16	12	53
3	Great Britain	14	7	8	29
4	Korea	9	3	5	17
5	France	8	6	8	22
6	Germany	5	10	6	21
7	Italy	5	5	3	13
8	Kazakhstan	5	0	0	5
9	DPR Korea	4	0	1	5
10	Russian Federation	3	15	10	28
11	Netherlands	3	1	4	8
12	South Africa	3	1	0	4
13	New Zealand	3	0	4	7
14	Japan	2	10	12	24
15	Cuba	2	2	1	5
16	Hungary	2	1	2	5
17	Poland	2	1	1	4
18	Ukraine	2	0	4	6
19	Australia	1	12	7	20
20	Romania	1	4	2	7
21	Canada	1	3	6	10
22	Belarus	1	2	3	6
23	Denmark	1	2	2	5
24	Czech Republic	1	2	1	4
25	Brazil	1	1	4	6
26	Croatia	1	1	0	2
27	Slovenia	1	0	2	3
28	Ethiopia	1	0	1	2
28	Jamaica	1	0	1	2
30	Switzerland	1	0	0	1
30	Venezuela	1	0	0	1
30	Georgia	1	0	0	1
30	Lithuania	1	0	0	1
34	Mexico	0	3	1	4
35	Sweden	0	3	0	3
36	Spain	0	2	1	3
36	Colombia	0	2	1	3
38	Slovakia	0	1	3	4
39	India	0	1	2	3
40	Kenya	0	1	1	2
40	Mongolia	0	1	1	2
40	Indonesia	0	1	1	2
40	Norway	0	1	1	2
40	Serbia	0	1	1	2
40	Belgium	0	1	1	2
46	Thailand	0	1	0	1
46	Taiwan	0	1	0	1
46	Egypt	0	1	0	1
46	Guatemala	0	1	0	1
50	Greece	0	0	2	2
50	Moldova	0	0	2	2
52	Azerbaijan	1	0	0	1
52	Uzbekistan	0	0	1	1
52	Tunisia	0	0	1	1
52	Qatar	0	0	1	1
52	Hong Kong	0	0	1	1
52	Iran	0	0	1	1
52	Singapore	0	0	1	1

141

Guatemala become the 141st National Olympic Committee to win an Olympic medal, after Erick Barrondo wins silver in the men's 20km Race Walk

6955

Number of points Great Britain's Jessica Ennis accumulates in the Heptathlon – the third highest in Olympic history

Having blown her medal chances at Beijing 2008 with her final shot, USA's Jamie Lynn Gray is all smiles after winning the women's Shooting 50m Rifle 3 Positions final with an Olympic record

Day 9

Usain Bolt puts any doubts aside that he is still the fastest man on the planet with a blistering 9.63sec victory in the 100m final. Training partner Yohan Blake is second, with USA's Justin Gatlin third

Lightning strikes twice

After a false start at the World Championships final last year, defending 100m champion Usain Bolt has a point to prove in the blue riband event of the Olympic Games. The Jamaican faces strong competition from countrymen Yohan Blake and Asafa Powell, plus Tyson Gay and Justin Gatlin of USA. But, despite a slow start, Bolt powers home in an Olympic record of 9.63sec, with Blake second in a personal best-equalling 9.75.

As Bolt holds his signature pose and celebrates with a hysterical London crowd, a legend is made.

Meanwhile, after an emotional defeat in the final of the Wimbledon tennis tournament just weeks before, Great Britain's Andy Murray has his eyes firmly on the gold medal in the Tennis men's Singles final against Swiss great Roger Federer. With poise and determination, Murray claims a stunning 6-2 6-1 6-4 victory in under two hours.

At Weymouth and Portland, Great Britain's Ben Ainslie becomes the most decorated Olympic sailor in history with his fourth consecutive gold medal as he triumphs in the men's Finn.

Badminton

China's **Dan Lin** becomes the first man to retain the Singles title at an Olympic Games, defeating rival Lee Chong Wei of Malaysia in a three-set classic

Cycling – Track

Denmark's **Lasse Norman Hansen** recovers from a mid-race crash in the 15km scratch race to take gold in a gripping Men's Omnium

Badminton

Cai Yun and **Fu Haifeng** beat Danes Mathias Boe and Carsten Mogensen in the men's Doubles final to complete China's clean sweep of Badminton golds

Diving

China's **Minxia Wu** picks up her second gold as she wins the women's 3m Springboard event by a comfortable margin of 34.8 poi

Great Britain's Louis Smith gains a silver in the men's Pommel Horse final after finishing level for gold with Hungary's Krisztian Berki – only to be edged out by Berki's higher execution score

Quote of the day

'Of course, it's an amazing feeling to represent your country. I hope there will be many more medals to come, because I really love the tune of our national anthem'

Romanian Vault gold medallist gymnast, Sandra Raluca Izbasa

Defending women's 400m champion Christine Ohuruogu produces an outstanding late charge in the final to claim a silver medal behind USA's Sanya Richards-Ross

Athletics

Olga Rypakova helps Kazakhstan to their sixth gold medal of the Games as she wins the women's Triple Jump with a best leap of 14.98m

Boxing

Women's Boxing is introduced into the Olympic programme for the first time with the Fly Weight bout between **Elena Savelyeva** of Russian Federation and DPR Korea's **Kim Hye Song**

Athletics

South Africa's **Oscar Pistorius** achieves his Olympic dream by competing in the semi-finals of the 400m after finishing second in his heat. Pistorius is the first double amputee to compete in the Olympic Games

★
Star of the day
Andy Murray

Less than a month after losing in the Wimbledon final to Roger Federer, Great Britain's Andy Murray takes the spoils in the Tennis men's Singles final against the Swiss world No.1, claiming his first Olympic gold medal. In front of a packed Centre Court crowd, Murray needed only three sets and 1hr 56min to win 6-2 6-1 6-4.

Andy Murray shows his delight after serving an ace to secure the men's Singles gold medal on Wimbledon's Centre Court. The Scot later wins silver in the Mixed Doubles final alongside 18-year-old Laura Robson

Defending champions **Iain Percy** and **Andrew 'Bart' Simpson** are pipped on the line as the Britons take Star silver behind surprise winners Freddie Loof and Max Salminen of Sweden

Korea's **Jong-Oh Jin** claims his second gold of the Games with victory in the men's 50m Pistol. His final shot lifts the defending champion above compatriot Young-Rae Choi, who takes silver

USA's gold medal favourite **McKayla Maroney** suffers a surprise defeat in the Vault final after making an error on her second effort, allowing Romania's Sandra Izbasa to claim the top prize

Day 9, 5 August

Who won the medals today

Afternoon
Shooting
Men's 50m Pistol
- Jong-Oh Jin (KOR)............................662.0
- Young-Rae Choi (KOR) 661.5
- Zhiwei Wang (CHN) 658.6

Afternoon
Tennis
Mixed Doubles
- Victoria Azarenka/
Max Mirnyi (BEL) 2, 6, 10
- Andy Murray/
Laura Robson (GBR) 6, 3, 8
- Lisa Raymond/
Mike Bryan (USA) 6-3, 4-6, 10-4

Afternoon
Athletics
Women's Marathon
- Tiki Gelana (ETH)........................2:23.07
- Priscah Jeptoo (KEN) 2:23.12
- Tatyana Petrova Arkhipova (RUS) 2:23.29

Afternoon
Sailing
Men's Star
- Fredrik Loof/Max Salminen (SWE)........32
- Iain Percy/Andrew Simpson (GBR)........34
- Robert Scheidt/Bruno Prada (BRA) 40

Afternoon
Badminton
Men's Singles
- Dan Lin (CHN).........................15, 21, 21
- Chong Wei Lee (MAS)...............21, 10, 19
- Long Chen (CHN) 21-12, 15-21, 21-15

Afternoon
Gymnastics – Artistic
Men's Floor Exercise
- Kai Zou (CHN) 15.933
- Kohei Uchimura (JPN)..................15.800
- Denis Ablyazin (RUS) 15.800

Afternoon
Sailing
Men's Finn
- Ben Ainslie (GBR)................................46
- Jonas Høgh-Christensen (DEN).............46
- Jonathan Lobert (FRA)........................49

Afternoon
Gymnastics – Artistic
Women's Vault
- Sandra Raluca Izbasa (ROU) 15.191
- McKayla Maroney (USA).............. 15.083
- Maria Paseka (RUS) 15.050

Afternoon
Badminton
Men's Doubles
- Yun Cai/Haifeng Fu (CHN) 21, 21
- Mathias Boe/
Carsten Mogensen (DEN) 16, 15
- Jae Sung Chung/
Yong Dae Lee (KOR)............. 23-21, 21-10

Afternoon
Gymnastics – Artistic
Men's Pommel Horse
- Krisztian Berki (HUN)...................16.066
- Louis Smith (GBR).......................16.066
- Max Whitlock (GBR) 15.600

Afternoon
Weightlifting
Women's + 75kg
- Lulu Zhou (CHN) 333kg
- Tatiana Kashirina (RUS) 332kg
- Hripsime Khurshudyan (ARM).........294kg

Afternoon
Tennis
Men's Singles
- Andy Murray (GBR)........................6, 6, 6
- Roger Federer (SUI) 2, 1, 4
- Juan Martin del Potro (ARG)........7-5, 6-4

Afternoon
Wrestling
Men's Greco-Roman 55kg
- Soryan Reihanpour (IRI).........................3
- Rovshan Bayramov (AZE)........................0
- Peter Modos (HUN)..........................3-1
- Mingiyan Semenov (RUS)....................3-1

Afternoon
Cycling Track
Men's Omnium
- Lasse Norman Hansen (DEN)...............27
- Bryan Coquard (FRA) 29
- Edward Clancy (GBR)........................30

Afternoon
Tennis
Women's Doubles
- Serena Williams/
Venus Williams (USA)........................6, 6
- Andrea Hlavackova/
Lucie Hradecka (CZE)........................4, 4
- Maria Kirilenko/
Nadia Petrova (RUS) 4-6, 6-4, 6-1

Evening
Wrestling
Men's Greco-Roman 74kg
- Roman Vlasov (RUS) 3
- Arsen Julfalakyan (ARM)........................0
- Aleksandr Kazakevic (LTU)..................3-0
- Emin Ahmadov (AZE) 3-1

Evening
Fencing
Men's Team Foil
- Italy 45
- Japan 39
- Germany.......................................45-27

Evening
Athletics
Women's Triple Jump
- Olga Rypakova (KAZ) 14.98
- Caterine Ibarguen (COL) 14.80
- Olha Saladuha (UKR) 14.79

Evening
Athletics
Women's 400m
- Sanya Richards-Ross (USA) 49.55
- Christine Ohuruogu (GBR) 49.70
- DeeDee Trotter (USA) 49.72

Evening
Athletics
Men's 3000m Steeplechase
- Ezekiel Kemboi (KEN) 8:18.56
- Mahiedine Mekhissi-
Benabbad (FRA) 8:19.08
- Abel Kiprop Mutai (KEN).............8:19.73

Evening
Athletics
Men's Hammer Throw
- Krisztian Pars (HUN) 80.59
- Primoz Kozmus (SLO)....................79.36
- Koji Murofushi (JPN)......................78.71

Evening
Athletics
Men's 100m
- Usain Bolt (JAM) 9.63
- Yohan Blake (JAM)...........................9.75
- Justin Gatlin (USA) 9.79

Evening
Diving
Women's 3m Springboard
- Minxia Wu (CHN) 414.00
- Zi He (CHN)...............................379.20
- Laura Sanchez Soto (MEX)............362.40

Ben Ainslie holds his nerve at Weymouth and Portland to sail into the history books as the most successful Olympic sailor of all time. This is the Briton's fourth consecutive gold and third in the Finn class

Usain Bolt is projected on to London's Houses of Parliament following his historic victory in the 100m final

10.00s
Seven of the eight 100m finalists run under 10 seconds – a record at an Olympic Games

Iran's **Soryan Reihanpour** wins a benchmark gold in the 55kg Greco-Roman final, the first Wrestling medal awarded at the 2012 Games. The gold is also the first ever for his country in the discipline and makes him Iran's first Olympic champion at London 2012

AINSLIE

GBR

London 2012

Medal table

The peak audience on BBC TV for Usain Bolt's win in the 100m final

20,000,000

1	China	30	17	14	61
2	USA	28	14	18	60
3	Great Britain	16	11	10	37
4	Korea	10	4	6	20
5	France	8	8	9	25
6	Italy	6	5	3	14
7	Kazakhstan	6	0	0	6
8	Germany	5	10	7	22
9	Russian Federation	4	16	15	35
10	Hungary	4	1	3	8
11	DPR Korea	4	0	1	5
12	Netherlands	3	1	4	8
13	South Africa	3	1	0	4
14	New Zealand	3	0	4	7
15	Japan	2	12	13	27
16	Denmark	2	4	2	8
16	Romania	2	4	2	8
18	Belarus	2	2	3	7
19	Cuba	2	2	1	5
20	Jamaica	2	1	1	4
20	Poland	2	1	1	4
22	Ukraine	2	0	5	7
23	Ethiopia	2	0	1	3
24	Australia	1	12	7	20
25	Canada	1	3	6	10
26	Czech Republic	1	3	1	5
27	Sweden	1	3	0	4
28	Kenya	1	2	2	5
29	Brazil	1	1	5	7
30	Slovenia	1	1	2	4
31	Croatia	1	1	0	2
31	Switzerland	1	1	0	2
33	Iran	1	0	1	2
33	Lithuania	1	0	1	2
35	Georgia	1	0	0	1
35	Venezuela	1	0	0	1
37	Mexico	0	3	2	5
38	Colombia	0	3	1	4
39	Spain	0	2	1	3
40	Slovakia	0	1	3	4
41	Azerbaijan	0	1	2	3
41	India	0	1	2	3
43	Armenia	0	1	1	2
43	Belgium	0	1	1	2
43	Indonesia	0	1	1	2
43	Mongolia	0	1	1	2
43	Norway	0	1	1	2
43	Serbia	0	1	1	2
49	Egypt	0	1	0	1
49	Guatemala	0	1	0	1
49	Malaysia	0	1	0	1
49	Thailand	0	1	0	1
49	Taipei (Chinese Taipei)	0	1	0	1
54	Greece	0	0	2	2
54	Republic of Moldova	0	0	2	2
56	Argentina	0	0	1	1
56	Hong Kong	0	0	1	1
56	Qatar	0	0	1	1
56	Singapore	0	0	1	1
56	Tunisia	0	0	1	1
56	Uzbekistan	0	0	1	1

1920

The last time Great Britain won Olympic gold in Tennis before Andy Murray's Singles triumph

1

Dan Lin (CHN) becomes the first player to retain the Badminton men's Singles title at the Olympic Games

5

Krisztian Pars hands Hungary their fifth gold medal in men's Hammer Throw, and the first since Balazs Kiss in 1996

Police officers near the Olympic Stadium pay tribute to 100m champion Usain Bolt

Day 10

British riders jump for joy

In front of a capacity 23,000 crowd at Greenwich Park, Great Britain win their first Olympic Equestrian – Jumping title for 60 years as Scott Brash, Peter Charles, Ben Maher and Nick Skelton claim gold in the Team Competition. Skelton, riding Big Star, Maher (Tripple X III) and Charles (Vindicat) all jump clear to land the top prize, leaving Netherlands with silver, while Saudi Arabia take bronze.

At the Velodrome, Great Britain's dominance continues with Jason Kenny edging out France's Gregory Baugé to win the men's Sprint final.

As Kenny becomes the first British man to win two medals in the Cycling sprints at a Games, following his silver at Beijing 2008, Beth Tweddle wins her first Olympic medal as she finishes third in the women's Uneven Bars competition.

In the evening session at the Olympic Stadium, Dominican Republic's Felix Sanchez rounds off an action-packed Day 10 by becoming the oldest medallist in the 400m Hurdles at the Olympic Games, topping the podium. The 34-year-old reclaims the crown eight years after winning gold at Athens 2004.

In a nail-biting conclusion to the Team Competition, Great Britain's Nick Skelton, Ben Maher, Chris Brash and Peter Charles defeat Netherlands in a jump-off to take the gold medal

Gymnastics – Artistic

Brazilian gymnast **Arthur Nabarrete Zanetti** causes a major upset by taking the gold in the Rings Competition final, beating hot favourite and defending Olympic champion Chen Yibing of China. Italy's Matteo Morandi wins the bronze

Wrestling

World champion, 21-year-old **Roman Vlasov** of Russian Federation, takes gold in the 74kg Greco-Roman Wrestling final, beating Armenia's Arsen Julfalakyan

Synchronised Swimming

Jenna Randall and **Olivia Federici** claim the first British spot in a Synchronised Swimming final since 1992, as they clinch ninth place in the preliminary rounds

★

Star of the day

Jason Kenny

On the penultimate day of competition in the Velodrome, it's down to Jason Kenny to continue Great Britain's dominance in the men's Sprint. Setting the fastest qualifying time, the 24-year-old makes light work of Frenchman Gregory Baugé, winning 2-0 in the final. The gold is Kenny's third, but his first in individual competition. Great Britain now have five gold medals in seven Track Cycling events, with three more to be contested on Day 11.

Hockey

A surprise 1-0 victory for Japan over China secures a first Olympic Games semi-final appearance in 20 years for **Great Britain's** women's Hockey team

Athletics

Defending champion **Yelena Isinbayeva** of Russian Federation is beaten to gold in a tight women's Pole Vault final. A 4.75m clearance by USA's Jennifer Suhr wins gold on countback from Cuba's Yarisley Silva. Isinbayeva takes the bronze

Cycling — Track

Laura Trott wins two of her three events on day one of the Omnium. The Briton goes into day two tied on points with Sarah Hammer of USA in the overall rankings

Jason Kenny savours the adulation of the Velodrome crowd after following in the footsteps of compatriot Sir Chris Hoy by winning the men's Sprint. Gregory Baugé of France takes silver, with Australia's Shane Perkins claiming the bronze

Football

A last-minute extra-time winner from **Alex Morgan** earns USA a dramatic 4-3 victory over North American rivals Canada to book a spot in the Olympic women's final

Boxing

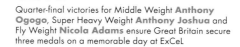

Quarter-final victories for Middle Weight **Anthony Ogogo**, Super Heavy Weight **Anthony Joshua** and Fly Weight **Nicola Adams** ensure Great Britain secure three medals on a memorable day at ExCeL

Athletics

Nineteen-year-old **Kirani James** runs a superb race to add Olympic 400m gold to his world title. Completing the one lap in a blistering 43.94sec, James becomes the first Grenadian to win a medal in Olympic history

Day 10, 6 August

Who won the medals today

Afternoon
Shooting
Men's 50m Rifle 3 Position
- Niccolo Campriani (ITA) 1278.5
- Jonghyun Kim (KOR) 1272.5
- Matthew Emmons (USA) 1271.3

Afternoon
Sailing
Women's Laser Radial
- Lijia Xu (CHN) 35
- Marit Bouwmeester (NED) 37
- Evi van Acker (BEL).............................40

Afternoon
Sailing
Men's Laser
- Tom Slingsby (AUS) 43
- Pavlos Kontides (CYP)........................59
- Rasmus Myrgren (SWE) 72

Afternoon
Gymnastics – Artistic
Men's Rings Competition
- Arthur Nabarrete Zanetti (BRA) 15.900
- Yibing Chen (CHN)...................... 15.800
- Matteo Morandi (ITA) 15.733

Afternoon
Gymnastics – Artistic
Women's Uneven Bars Competition
- Aliya Mustafina (RUS).................. 16.133
- Kexin He (CHN)........................... 15.933
- Elizabeth Tweddle (GBR) 15.916

Afternoon
Gymnastics – Artistic
Men's Vault Competition
- Hak-Seon Yang (KOR) 16.533
- Denis Ablyazin (RUS) 16.399
- Igor Radivilov (UKR) 16.316

Afternoon
Equestrian
Jumping Team Competition
- Great Britain
- Netherlands
- Saudi Arabia

Afternoon
Shooting
Men's Trap
- Giovanni Cernogoraz (CRO).............. 146
- Massimo Fabbrizi (ITA).................... 146
- Fehaid Aldeehani (KUW)................... 145

Afternoon
Cycling – Track
Men's Sprint
- Jason Kenny (GBR) 2
- Gregory Baugé (FRA) 0
- Shane Perkins (AUS) 2-0

Afternoon
Wrestling
Men's Greco-Roman 60kg
- Omid Haji Noroozi (IRI) 3
- Revaz Lashkhi (GEO) 0
- Zaur Kuramagomedov (RUS) 3-0
- Ryutaro Matsumoto (JPN)..................5-0

Evening
Wrestling
Men's Greco-Roman 84kg
- Alan Khugaev (RUS) 3
- Karam Mohamed Gaber Ebrahim (EGY)..0
- Danyal Gajiyev (KAZ) 3-1
- Damian Janikowski (POL) 3-0

Evening
Wrestling
Men's Greco-Roman 120kg
- Mijain Lopez Nunez (CUB) 3
- Heiki Nabi (EST) 0
- Riza Kayaalp (TUR) 3-0
- Johan Euren (SWE)............................3-1

Evening
Athletics
Women's Shot Put
- Nadzeya Ostapchuk (BLR) 21.36
- Valerie Adams (NZL) 20.70
- Evgeniia Kolodko (RUS) 20.48

Evening
Athletics
Men's 400m Hurdles
- Felix Sanchez (DOM) 47.63
- Michael Tinsley (USA) 47.91
- Javier Culson (PUR) 48.10

Evening
Weightlifting
Men's 105kg
- Oleksiy Torokhtiy (UKR) 412kg
- Navab Nasirshelal (IRI) 411kg
- Bartlomiej Wojciech Bonk (POL)......410kg

Evening
Athletics
Women's 3000m Steeplechase
- Yuliya Zaripova (RUS)...................9:06.72
- Habiba Ghribi (TUN) 9:08.37
- Sofia Assefa (ETH) 9:09.84

Evening
Athletics
Men's 400m
- Kirani James (GRN) 43.94
- Luguelin Santos (DOM)................. 44.46
- Lalonde Gordon (TRI) 44.52

Evening
Athletics
Women's Pole Vault
- Jennifer Suhr (USA) 4.75m
- Yarisley Silva (CUB) 4.75m
- Elena Isinbaeva (RUS)................... 4.70m

Great Britain's Beth Tweddle puts the last 40 seconds of her routine to excellent use, winning her first Olympic medal – a bronze in the Individual Uneven Bars. Former All-Around world champion Aliya Mustafina takes gold

60

The number of years since Team Jumping winners Great Britain last won an Equestrian gold

1

Habiba Ghribi wins the first medal by a Tunisian woman in Olympic history as she takes silver in the 3000m Steeplechase

Great Britain's men end their Olympic Games in style with their first win in the Basketball tournament – a 90-58 win over China. Kieron Achara is the top scorer with 16 points

600

The number of basketballs used during Games time at London 2012

Nobody could have predicted the unlikely outcome in the 400m Hurdles, where the 2004 Olympic champion Felix Sanchez of Dominican Republic claims gold in exactly the same time he ran in Athens – 47.63sec

Sailing

Tom Slingsby restores some Australian pride, earning the nation its second gold medal of the Games by winning the men's Laser class. In taking silver Pavlos Kontides becomes Cyprus's first Olympic medallist since the nation's independence 52 years ago

Quote of the day

'I like pressure. Diamonds are made under pressure'

Australian BMX rider Caroline Buchanan plans a sparkling Games

1928

The last time Great Britain won a medal in women's Gymnastics, before Beth Tweddle takes bronze in the women's Uneven Bars Competition. It is also Great Britain's first individual medal in the event

The victorious Jumping Team Competition foursome line up to receive Great Britain's 17th gold medal of the Games

34 years 342 days

Felix Sanchez (DOM) wins the 400m Hurdles, becoming the oldest gold medallist in a men's sprint event (400m and shorter) at an Olympic Games

Medal table

1	China	31	19	14	64
2	USA	29	15	19	63
3	Great Britain	18	11	11	40
4	Korea	11	5	6	22
5	France	8	9	9	26
6	Russian Federation	7	17	18	42
7	Italy	7	6	4	17
8	Kazakhstan	6	0	1	7
9	Germany	5	10	7	22
10	Hungary	4	1	3	8
11	DPR Korea	4	0	1	5
12	Netherlands	3	3	4	10
13	Cuba	3	3	1	7
14	Belarus	3	2	3	8
15	New Zealand	3	1	4	8
16	South Africa	3	1	0	4
17	Ukraine	3	0	6	9
18	Japan	2	12	14	28
19	Australia	2	12	8	22
20	Denmark	2	4	2	8
20	Romania	2	4	2	8
22	Brazil	2	1	5	8
23	Poland	2	1	3	6
24	Iran	2	1	1	4
24	Jamaica	2	1	1	4
26	Croatia	2	1	0	3
27	Ethiopia	2	0	2	4
28	Canada	1	3	6	10
29	Sweden	1	3	2	6
30	Czech Republic	1	3	1	5
31	Kenya	1	2	2	5
32	Slovenia	1	1	2	4
33	Dominican Republic	1	1	0	2
33	Georgia	1	1	0	2
33	Switzerland	1	1	0	2
36	Lithuania	1	0	1	2
37	Grenada	1	0	0	1
37	Venezuela	1	0	0	1
39	Mexico	0	3	2	5
40	Colombia	0	3	1	4
41	Spain	0	2	1	3
42	Egypt	0	2	0	2
43	Slovakia	0	1	3	4
44	Azerbaijan	0	1	2	3
44	Belgium	0	1	2	3
44	India	0	1	2	3
47	Armenia	0	1	1	2
47	Indonesia	0	1	1	2
47	Mongolia	0	1	1	2
47	Norway	0	1	1	2
47	Serbia	0	1	1	2
47	Tunisia	0	1	1	2
53	Cyprus	0	1	0	1
53	Estonia	0	1	0	1
53	Guatemala	0	1	0	1
53	Malaysia	0	1	0	1
53	Thailand	0	1	0	1
53	Taipei (Chinese Taipei)	0	1	0	1
59	Greece	0	0	2	2
59	Republic of Moldova	0	0	2	2
61	Argentina	0	0	1	1
61	Hong Kong, China	0	0	1	1
61	Saudi Arabia	0	0	1	1
61	Kuwait	0	0	1	1
61	Puerto Rico	0	0	1	1
61	Qatar	0	0	1	1
61	Singapore	0	0	1	1
61	Trinidad and Tobago	0	0	1	1
61	Turkey	0	0	1	1
61	Uzbekistan	0	0	1	1

Sir Chris Hoy becomes the greatest British Olympian in history by landing a sixth Olympic gold medal with a frenetic dash for the line in the men's Track Cycling Keirin final

Day 11

Tears of Hoy

It's a landmark day for Great Britain as Team GB surpasses its Beijing 2008 medal haul of 47 and further cements its third place spot in the medal table behind China and USA.

Sir Chris Hoy and Laura Trott win their second gold medals of London 2012 as Britain equalled their Beijing 2008 Track Cycling haul of seven wins from 10 events. An emotional Sir Chris wins the men's Keirin to claim his sixth gold medal, propelling him to superstardom with more gold medals to his name than Sir Steve Redgrave.

Hoy's win provides even more inspiration for Trott, who takes her second gold of the Games by winning the women's Omnium.

The Triathlon becomes a family affair as brothers Alistair and Jonny Brownlee take gold and bronze respectively after a show-stopping performance at Hyde Park.

Meanwhile, Greenwich Park is the scene of more celebrations for Britain as the Equestrian – Dressage team of Carl Hester, Laura Bechtolsheimer and Charlotte Dujardin continue the winning streak, beating favourites Germany to take gold.

Diving

Russia's **Ilya Zakharov** causes a huge upset in the Diving world as he stops China's clean sweep of the London 2012 golds in its tracks by topping the podium in the 3m Springboard final

Gymnastics — Artistic

Aly Raisman (USA) takes gold in the women's Floor Exercise, stopping the Romanian team from winning the event for a third consecutive Games

Weightlifting

Iran take a one-two in the men's Super Heavyweight division (+105kg). **Behdad Salimikordasiabi** wins gold with a total lift of 455kg. It is the third Olympic Games in which Iran have taken this title

★
Star of the day
Epke Zonderland

In the final of the men's Horizontal Bar, it would take something special to upset the odds, as defending champion Kai Zou (China) and Fabian Hambuchen (Germany) enter the competition as favourites. Much of the talk before the event is centred around Dutchman Epke Zonderland, who would gamble on a difficult routine to break into the medal places. High risk, high reward.

Combining three release moves – the Cassina, the Kovacs and the Kolman – one after the other, Zonderland becomes the first gymnast to perform a triple flight combination at the Olympic Games. He lands his dismount expertly and, with a score of 16.533 (7.9 in difficulty and 8.633 execution) takes gold – Netherlands' first ever medal in the men's competition.

Athletics

Germany's **Robert Harting** wins gold in the men's Discus Throw with 68.27m. Afterwards, he leaps over every hurdle laid out for the women's 100m Hurdles final while wrapped in his national flag

Cycling — Track

Victoria Pendleton's last race before retirement ends in disappointment as she is beaten to gold 2-0 in the women's Sprint final by her Australian rival Anna Meares. Pendleton adds a silver medal to the gold she won in the women's Keirin

Athletics

Andrew Osagie of Great Britain finishes second in his semi-final behind world record holder David Rudisha (KEN) to qualify for the men's 800m final

Team GB's Nick Dempsey improves on his fourth place finish at Beijing 2008 to take silver in the men's Sailing RS:X at Weymouth and Portland

Russian Federation continues its dominance in the Synchronised Swimming Duet event as Natalia Ishchenko and Svetlana Romashina astounded the London 2012 judges and topped the podium

Quote of the day

'This colour I did not have actually. I only have three gold and five silvers, so my collection is done'

Three-time Equestrian Dressage champion Anky Van Grunsven (NED) completes his medal set by taking bronze at Greenwich Park

Laura Trott wins her second Track Cycling gold medal of the London 2012 Games with victory in the women's Omnium. A scintillating ride in the 500m time trial – the final event of the competition – secures her victory

Football

Brazil are on their way to the final against Mexico after a convincing 3-0 win against Korea at Old Trafford. Having scored 15 goals in five games, the Brazilians have their sights set on their first Olympic gold in the sport

Hockey

Great Britain's men reach their first semi-final at an Olympic Games for 24 years as they claim a nervy 1-1 draw against Spain at the Riverbank Arena

Athletics

Sally Pearson of Australia sets an Olympic record of 12.35sec to win a thrilling women's 100m Hurdles final by just 0.02sec from the Beijing 2008 champion Dawn Harper (USA)

Day 11, 7 August

Who won the medals today

Afternoon
Triathlon
Men's
● Alistair Brownlee (GBR) 1:46.25
● Javier Gomez (ESP) 1:46.36
● Jonathan Brownlee (GBR) 1:46.56

Afternoon
Sailing
RS:X Men's
● Dorian van Rijsselberge (NED) 15
● Nick Dempsey (GBR) 41
● Przemyslaw Miarczynski (POL) 60

Afternoon
Gymnastics Artistic
Men's Parallel Bars Competition
● Feng Zhe (CHN) 15.966
● Marcel Nguyen (GER) 15.800
● Hamilton Sabot (FRA) 15.566

Afternoon
Sailing
RS:X Women's
● Marina Alabau Neira (ESP) 26
● Tuuli Petaja (FIN) 46
● Zofia Noceti-Klepacka (POL) 47

Afternoon
Gymnastics – Artistic
Women's Balance Beam Competition
● Linlin Deng (CHN) 15.600
● Lu Sui (CHN) 15.500
● Alexandra Raisman (USA) 15.066

Afternoon
Gymnastics – Artistic
Men's Horizontal Bar Competition
● Epke Zonderland (NED) 16.533
● Fabian Hambuchen (GER) 16.400
● Kai Zou (CHN) 16.366

Afternoon
Synchronised Swimming
Duets
● Natalia Ishchenko/
Svetlana Romashina (RUS) 197.100
● Ona Carbonell Ballestero/
Andrea Fuentes Fache (ESP) 192.900
● Xuechen Huang/Ou Liu (CHN).... 192.870

Afternoon
Equestrian
Dressage Team Competition
● Great Britain 79.979
● Germany...................................... 78.216
● Netherlands 78.216

Afternoon
Gymnastics – Artistic
Women's Floor Competition
● Alexandra Raisman (USA)............. 15.600
● Catalina Ponor (ROU)................... 15.200
● Aliya Mustafina (RUS)................... 14.900

Afternoon
Cycling – Track
Women's Omnium
● Laura Trott (GBR)................................ 18
● Sarah Hammer (USA)........................... 19
● Annette Edmondson (AUS) 24

Afternoon
Cycling – Track
Men's Keirin
● Sir Chris Hoy (GBR)..................... 10.306
● Maximilian Levy (GER) .... n/a
● Simon van Velthooven (NZL) .... n/a
● Teun Mulder (NED) .... n/a

Afternoon
Cycling – Track
Women's Sprint
● Anna Meares (AUS) 2
● Victoria Pendleton (GBR)...................... 0
● Shuang Guo (CHN) 2-0

Afternoon
Table Tennis
Women's Team
● China 3
● Japan 0
● Singapore 3-0

Afternoon
Wrestling
Men's Greco-Roman 66kg
● Hyeon-Woo Kim (KOR)........................ 3
● Tamas Lorincz (HUN) 0
● Manuchar Tskhadaia (GEO) 3-1
● Steeve Guenot (FRA) 3-0

Evening
Wrestling
Men's Greco-Roman 96kg
● Ghasem Gholamreza Rezaei (IRI)...........3
● Rustam Totrov (RUS)...............................0
● Artur Aleksanyan (ARM) 3-0
● Jimmy Lidberg (SWE).........................3-1

Evening
Athletics
Women's 100m Hurdles
● Sally Pearson (AUS) .... 12.35 (OR)
● Dawn Harper (USA) 12.37
● Kellie Wells (USA) 12.48

Evening
Athletics
Men's Discus Throw
● Robert Harting (GER)................... 68.27m
● Ehsan Hadadi (IRI) 68.18m
● Gerd Kanter (EST) 68.03m

Evening
Athletics
Men's High Jump
● Ivan Ukhov (RUS) 2.38m
● Erik Kynard (USA) 2.33m
● Mutaz Essa Barshim (QAT)............ 2.29m
● Derek Drouin (CAN) 2.29m
● Robert Grabarz (GBR) 2.29m

Evening
Athletics
Men's 1500m
● Taoufik Makhloufi (ALG) 3:34.08
● Leonel Manzano (USA)................. 3:34.79
● Abdalaati Iguider (MAR) 3:35.13

Evening
Weightlifting
Men's +105kg
● Behdad Salimikordasiabi (IRI) 455kg
● Sajjad Anoushiravani Hamlabad (IRI)449kg
● Ruslan Albegov (RUS) 448kg

Evening
Diving
Men's 3m Springboard
● Ilya Zakharov (RUS)..................... 555.90
● Kai Qin (CHN) 541.75
● Chong He (CHN) 524.15

Carl Hester, Laura Bechtolsheimer and Charlotte Dujardin win Great Britain's first Equestrian – Dressage medal at an Olympic Games by taking the Team Competition gold

749 & 750

Alistair Brownlee's gold and Jonny Brownlee's bronze in the men's Triathlon are Great Britain's 749th and 750th at the Olympic Games

2.38m

Ivan Ukhov (Russia) wins the High Jump with the highest jump since the 1996 Olympic Games

Wrestling

Ghasem Rezaei completes Iran's Wrestling hat-trick with gold in the men's Greco-Roman 96kg, fighting off Russian Federation's Rustam Totrov

Athletics

Robbie Grabarz (GBR) shares High Jump bronze with two other jumpers after clearing 2.29m. Russia's Ivan Ukhov clears 2.38m to take gold

The Brownlee brothers, Alistair and Jonny, secure gold and bronze medals in a thrilling men's Triathlon. It is the first time that two British siblings share a podium in the same individual event for 112 years

1928

The last time Netherlands won a medal in Artistic Gymnastics, before Epke Zonderland's gold in the Horizontal Bar

0

For the first time in Olympic history, USA's men's team return home without winning a single Boxing medal

Medal table

1	China	34	21	18	73
2	USA	30	19	21	70
3	Great Britain	22	13	13	48
4	Korea	12	5	6	23
5	Russian Federation	10	18	20	48
6	France	8	9	11	28
7	Italy	7	6	4	17
8	Germany	6	14	7	27
9	Kazakhstan	6	0	1	7
10	Netherlands	5	3	6	14
11	Australia	4	12	9	25
12	Islamic Republic of Iran	4	3	1	8
13	Hungary	4	2	3	9
14	DPR Korea	4	0	1	5
15	Cuba	3	3	1	7
16	Belarus	3	2	3	8
17	New Zealand	3	1	5	9
18	South Africa	3	1	0	4
19	Ukraine	3	0	6	9
20	Japan	2	13	14	29
21	Romania	2	5	2	9
22	Denmark	2	4	2	8
23	Brazil	2	1	5	8
23	Poland	2	1	5	8
25	Jamaica	2	1	1	4
26	Croatia	2	1	0	3
27	Ethiopia	2	0	2	4
28	Spain	1	4	1	6
29	Canada	1	3	7	11
30	Sweden	1	3	3	7
31	Czech Republic	1	3	1	5
32	Kenya	1	2	2	5
33	Slovenia	1	1	2	4
34	Georgia	1	1	1	3
35	Dominican Republic	1	1	0	2
35	Switzerland	1	1	0	2
37	Lithuania	1	0	1	2
38	Algeria	1	0	0	1
38	Grenada	1	0	0	1
38	Venezuela	1	0	0	1
41	Mexico	0	3	2	5
42	Colombia	0	3	1	4
43	Egypt	0	2	0	2
44	Slovakia	0	1	3	4
45	Armenia	0	1	2	3
45	Azerbaijan	0	1	2	3
45	Belgium	0	1	2	3
45	India	0	1	2	3
49	Estonia	0	1	1	2
49	Indonesia	0	1	1	2
49	Mongolia	0	1	1	2
49	Norway	0	1	1	2
49	Serbia	0	1	1	2
49	Tunisia	0	1	1	2
55	Cyprus	0	1	0	1
55	Finland	0	1	0	1
55	Guatemala	0	1	0	1
55	Malaysia	0	1	0	1
55	Taipei (Chinese Taipei)	0	1	0	1
55	Thailand	0	1	0	1
61	Greece	0	0	2	2
61	Republic of Moldova	0	0	2	2
61	Qatar	0	0	2	2
61	Singapore	0	0	2	2
65	Argentina	0	0	1	1
65	Hong Kong, China	0	0	1	1
65	Kuwait	0	0	1	1
65	Morocco	0	0	1	1
65	Puerto Rico	0	0	1	1
65	Saudi Arabia	0	0	1	1
65	Trinidad and Tobago	0	0	1	1
65	Turkey	0	0	1	1
65	Uzbekistan	0	0	1	1

Aries Merritt (USA) storms to a personal best of 12.92sec to take 110m Hurdles gold. Britain's 22-year-old Lawrence Clarke has an outstanding race to finish fourth in 13.39 – just outside his best time of 13.31, set in the semi-final

Golden day for USA

For one night, the Olympic Stadium belongs to USA as they win three golds in the Athletics events. Allyson Felix takes gold in the women's 200m, with fellow American Carmelita Jeter finishing third.

Aries Merritt becomes the first American winner of the 110m Hurdles since 1996 as he storms to victory in 12.92sec – the fastest time in the world this year and just 0.01sec off the Olympic record.

Brittney Reese completes the hat-trick, becoming only the second American to win the women's Long Jump.

Meanwhile, Jamaica's Usain Bolt edges ever closer to legendary status as he eases into the 200m final. Team-mate Yohan Blake is the fastest qualifier after slowing down markedly in winning the opening semi-final in 20.01sec.

Elsewhere, Cycling BMX action gets under way with Great Britain's Shanaze Reade hoping home support inspires her after she crashed out in the final at Beijing 2008.

Day 12

Katalin Kovács of Hungary enhances her legendary status in Canoe Sprint with victory in the women's Kayak Four (K4) 500m alongside Gabriella Szabo, Danuta Kozak and Krisztina Fazekas, thus achieving her third Olympic gold

Italy dethrone defending Olympic champions USA by beating them 3-0 in the men's Volleyball quarter-final to book a place in the semi-final against two-time champions Brazil

Olympic silver medallists **Iceland**, who won all five pool games, go down to a shock 33-34 defeat to Hungary in their quarter-final at the Basketball Arena

Quote of the day

'I am fighting a guy who beat me 15-0 in Beijing. Our plan in the next fight is to score a point'

Irish boxer Paddy Barnes explains his tactics before meeting Zou Shiming (CHN) again in his next bout

Netherlands, the world No.1 women's Hockey side, win a dramatic 3-1 penalty shoot-out victory over New Zealand in the semi-final. The game had ended 2-2 after extra-time

Wrestling

Japan's **Kaori Icho** adds a third gold to her Olympic medal count as she defeats China's Jing Ruixue in the women's 63kg Freestyle final

Water Polo

Italy's men's team knock reigning Olympic champions Hungary out of gold-medal contention in the quarter-finals, preventing the Hungarians from claiming a fourth consecutive Olympic title

Taekwondo

Spain's **Joel Gonzalez Bonilla** wins the gold medal in the 58kg category with a fantastic head kick to Korea's Dae-Hoon Lee in the final. He is Spain's first Olympic champion at Taekwondo

Allyson Felix of the USA finally gets her hands on a gold medal with a brilliant run in the women's 200m final. Felix, runner-up at Athens 2004 and again at Beijing 2008, overcomes a sluggish start to clock a time of 21.88sec

★
Star of the day
Allyson Felix

Going into the final of the women's 200m, Felix knows history is not in her favour. At the age of 18, she came second in the event at Athens 2004, repeating the finish four years later in Beijing. Now 26, at her peak, it is surely her last chance for gold in her primary event.

Lining up against Jamaica's Shelly-Ann Fraser-Pryce, who won the 100m four days earlier, and fellow American and 100m silver medallist Carmelita Jeter, Felix needs to perform.

Starting poorly, Felix takes the initiative in the bend to lead into the straight and never looks back to finally win gold. She becomes the second woman in any sport in Olympic history to win an event for the first time after previously winning two silver medals in the same event.

Athletics

Sophie Hitchon delights a capacity crowd at the Olympic Stadium with a national record of 71.98m to advance to the final of the Hammer Throw

Sailing

Great Britain's women's 470 crew **Hannah Mills** and **Saskia Clark** are tied on 33 points with New Zealand. The teams will be battling it out for gold in a few days' time

Equestrian

Two members of Britain's Jumping Team champions **Nick Skelton** and **Scott Brash** go clear in the first of two final rounds of the Jumping Individual Competition at Greenwich Park. But they fall short, having fences down in the second round. Gold goes to Switzerland's Steve Guerdat

Day 12, 8 August

Who won the medals today

Morning
Canoe Sprint
Men's Kayak Single (K1) 1000m
- Eirik Veras Larsen (NOR) 3:26.462
- Adam van Koeverden (CAN) 3:27.170
- Max Hoff (GER) 3:27.759

Morning
Canoe Sprint
Men's Canoe Single (C1) 1000m
- Sebastian Brendel (GER)............. 3:47.176
- David Cal Figueroa (ESP)........... 3:48.053
- Mark Oldershaw (CAN) 3:48.502

Morning
Canoe Sprint
Men's Kayak Double (K2) 1000m
- Rudolf Dombi/
  Roland Kokeny (HUN) 3:09.646
- Fernando Pimenta/
  Emanuel Silva (POR).................. 3:09.699
- Martin Hollstein/
  Andreas Ihle (GER)..................... 3:10.117

Morning
Canoe Sprint
Women's Kayak Four (K4) 500m
- Hungary 1:30.827
- Germany.................................. 1:31.298
- Belarus 1:31.400

Afternoon
Sailing
Men's 49er
- Nathan Outteridge/Iain Jensen (AUS)...56
- Peter Burling/Blair Tuke (NZL) 80
- Allan Norregaard/Peter Lang (DEN)... 114

Afternoon
Equestrian
Jumping Individual Competition
- Steve Guerdat (SUI)..................................
- Gerco Schroder (NED) ....
- Cian O'Connor (IRL) ....

Afternoon
Table Tennis
Men's Team
- China 3
- Korea 0
- Germany...3-1

Afternoon
Wrestling
Women's 48kg Freestyle
- Hitomi Obara (JPN) 3
- Mariya Stadnyk (AZE) 1
- Carol Huynh (CAN) 3-0
- Clarissa Kyoko Mei Ling Chun (USA) ...3-0

Evening
Wrestling
Women's 63kg Freestyle
- Kaori Icho (JPN).....................................3
- Ruixue Jing (CHN)..................................0
- Battsetseg Soronzonbold (MGL) 3-0
- Lubov Volosova (RUS) 3-1

Evening
Athletics
Women's 400m Hurdles
- Natalya Antyukh (RUS)...................52.70
- Lashinda Demus (USA) 52.77
- Zuzana Hejnova (CZE) 53.38

Evening
Athletics
Women's 200m
- Allyson Felix (USA)........................ 21.88
- Shelly-Ann Fraser-Pryce (JAM)........22.09
- Carmelita Jeter (USA) 22.14

Evening
Athletics
Men's 110m Hurdles
- Aries Merritt (USA)........................ 12.92
- Jason Richardson (USA)................. 13.04
- Hansle Parchment (JAM)................13.12

Evening
Athletics
Women's Long Jump
- Brittney Reese (USA)....................... 7.12m
- Elena Sokolova (RUS) 7.07m
- Janay DeLoach (USA) 6.89m

Evening
Beach Volleyball
Women's Tournament
- Misty May-Treanor/
  Kerri Walsh Jennings (USA)....................2
- April Ross/Jennifer Kessy (USA).............0
- Larissa Franca/Juliana Silva (BRA)....... 2-1

Evening
Taekwondo
Women's -49kg
- Jingyu Wu (CHN) 8
- Brigitte Yague Enrique (ESP)................1
- Chanatip Sonkham (THA) 8-0
- Lucija Zaninovic (CRO) 6-5

Evening
Taekwondo
Men's -58kg
- Joel Gonzalez Bonilla (ESP) 17
- Dae-Hoon Lee (KOR) 8
- Alexey Denisenko (RUS)......................3-1
- Oscar Munoz Oviedo (COL) 6-4

Sarah Attar becomes the first Saudi Arabian woman to compete in the Olympic Games by running in the 800m heats

3
Kaori Icho (Japan) becomes the first Japanese woman to win three gold medals at the Olympic Games

100
Juliana and Larissa Franca win Brazil's 100th medal in its summer Olympic Games history, with bronze in the women's Beach Volleyball

8 August 1984
The USA wins two medals in three events – men's 100m Hurdles, women's 200m and women's long Jump – something that they last achieved on this day 28 years ago

Great Britain's hopes of a gold medal are dashed at the Riverbank Arena as the women's team go down to a 2-1 defeat to Argentina in the first semi-final. Great Britain now face New Zealand in the bronze medal match

356

The number of pairs of boxing gloves used at London 2012

Nicola Adams (left) makes history as Great Britain's first women's Boxing finalist at the Olympic Games. The Leeds-born fighter defeats Chungneijang Mery Kom Hmangte of India in her Fly Weight semi-final

Women's Beach Volleyball comes down to two teams from the USA. Misty May-Treanor and Kerri Walsh Jennings take the game in two sets to claim their third consecutive Olympic gold

21

The number of matches USA Beach Volleyball pair Kerri Walsh Jennings and Misty May-Treanor have won together at the Olympic Games

4,400,000

On Twitter there have been more than 4.4 million mentions of Team GB since the Games began (as of Day 12)

Medal table

1	China	36	22	19	77
2	USA	34	22	25	81
3	Great Britain	22	13	13	48
4	Korea	12	7	6	25
5	Russian Federation	11	19	23	53
6	Germany	8	15	10	33
7	France	8	9	11	28
8	Italy	7	6	4	17
9	Hungary	6	2	3	11
10	Kazakhstan	6	0	2	8
11	Australia	5	12	9	26
12	Netherlands	5	4	6	15
13	Japan	4	13	14	31
14	Islamic Republic of Iran	4	3	1	8
15	DPR Korea	4	0	1	5
16	Belarus	3	3	4	10
17	Cuba	3	3	1	7
18	New Zealand	3	2	5	10
19	South Africa	3	1	0	4
20	Ukraine	3	0	6	9
21	Spain	2	6	1	9
22	Romania	2	5	2	9
23	Denmark	2	4	3	9
24	Jamaica	2	2	2	6
25	Brazil	2	1	7	10
26	Poland	2	1	5	8
27	Croatia	2	1	1	4
28	Switzerland	2	1	0	3
29	Ethiopia	2	0	2	4
30	Canada	1	4	9	14
31	Sweden	1	3	3	7
32	Czech Republic	1	3	2	6
33	Kenya	1	2	2	5
34	Slovenia	1	1	2	4
35	Georgia	1	1	1	3
35	Norway	1	1	1	3
37	Dominican Republic	1	1	0	2
38	Lithuania	1	0	1	2
39	Algeria	1	0	0	1
39	Grenada	1	0	0	1
39	Venezuela	1	0	0	1
42	Colombia	0	3	2	5
42	Mexico	0	3	2	5
44	Azerbaijan	0	2	2	4
45	Egypt	0	2	0	2
46	India	0	1	3	4
46	Slovakia	0	1	3	4
48	Armenia	0	1	2	3
48	Belgium	0	1	2	3
48	Mongolia	0	1	2	3
51	Estonia	0	1	1	2
51	Indonesia	0	1	1	2
51	Serbia	0	1	1	2
51	Thailand	0	1	1	2
51	Tunisia	0	1	1	2
56	Cyprus	0	1	0	1
56	Finland	0	1	0	1
56	Guatemala	0	1	0	1
56	Malaysia	0	1	0	1
56	Portugal	0	1	0	1
56	Taipei (Chinese Taipei)	0	1	0	1
62	Greece	0	0	2	2
62	Republic of Moldova	0	0	2	2
62	Qatar	0	0	2	2
62	Singapore	0	0	2	2
66	Argentina	0	0	1	1
66	Hong Kong, China	0	0	1	1
66	Ireland	0	0	1	1
66	Saudi Arabia	0	0	1	1
66	Kuwait	0	0	1	1
66	Morocco	0	0	1	1
66	Puerto Rico	0	0	1	1
66	Tajikistan	0	0	1	1
66	Trinidad and Tobago	0	0	1	1
66	Turkey	0	0	1	1
66	Uzbekistan	0	0	1	1

Great Britain's Nicola Adams defeats No.1 seed Cancan Ren (CHN) in the Boxing Fly Weight (51kg) to become the first women's Olympic Boxing champion

Day 13

Girl power

It's a day to rewrite the history books. Great Britain's Nicola Adams becomes the first female boxer to win an Olympic gold medal after outclassing China's Ren Cancan in the Fly Weight final.

Soon afterward, Ireland's Boxing sensation Katie Taylor wins her country's first gold medal of London 2012 by beating Russian Federation's Sofya Ochigava.

Jade Jones seals a successful day for Team GB by winning their first ever Taekwondo gold, overcoming Hou Yuzhuo of China in the women's -57kg final.

A capacity 80,000 crowd at the Olympic Stadium sees Usain Bolt make history... again... as he becomes the first man to win the men's 100m and 200m sprints at two successive Olympic Games.

Earlier, Kenya's David Rudisha becomes the first athlete to set a world record on the track at London 2012 as he storms to 800m gold, stopping the clock at a remarkable 1:40.91.

After almost two hours of swimming in the Serpentine in Hyde Park, Britain's **Keri-Anne Payne** misses out on a medal in the 10km Marathon Swim by less than half a second

Insufficient winds at Weymouth and Portland delay Sailing. Great Britain's **Luke Patience** and **Stuart Bithell** are forced to wait to compete in the men's 470 Medal Race

In the 4 x 400m Relay heats, **Team GB** produce a season's best to make the final. Oscar Pistorius still has a chance of a historic medal as his South Africa team appeals and wins a place in the final, but the Jamaica squad fail to qualify

Quote of the day

'As soon as I took the first step past the 200m mark I felt it break. I heard it. I even put out a little war cry'

American Manteo Mitchell (left) on finishing his 4 x 400m Relay stint despite breaking his left fibula during the race

Great Britain's Charlotte Dujardin and her horse Valegro win their second Dressage gold of these Olympic Games with a routine set to movie theme tunes. Adelinde Cornelissen (NED) is second with fellow Briton Laura Bechtolsheimer winning the bronze medal

Germany's **Peter Kretschmer** and **Kurt Kuschela** take gold in the Canoe Double (C2) ahead of 2008 champions Andrei and Aliaksandr Bahdanovich (BLR)

After withstanding heavy pressure throughout the bronze medal match, **Canada's** women score deep into injury-time to beat France 1-0. The goal, scored by Diana Matheson, hands Canada their first medal in the women's Football Tournament

Katie Taylor is victorious over Russian Federation's Sofya Ochigava to give Ireland their first gold medal of London 2012. Taylor, a four-time world champion, digs deep in the Light Weight (60kg) final to defeat her rival 10-8

David Rudisha runs an electric race, setting a new world record in the men's 800m final. Trained by an Irish priest, managed by an Australian and residing in Germany, the Kenyan runner is the toast of London

★
Star of the day
Usain Bolt

Usain Bolt secures the legendary status he's been craving as he becomes the first man to win the Olympic Games sprint double twice in succession.

The Jamaican establishes a clear lead within a few strides, but countryman Yohan Blake quickly pursues, closing the gap with 100m to go before Bolt turns on the after-burners and crosses the line in 19.32sec. After the race, Bolt declares: 'Loads of people were talking, but they can stop talking – I am a legend'.

Cycling — BMX

After recovering from a serious collarbone fracture only a few months ago, **Liam Phillips** (GBR) comes back fighting with a solid display in the seeding runs. He qualifies for the semi-finals and looks confident

Athletics

Usain Bolt wins the men's 200m final in a season's best 19.32sec. Yohan Blake takes silver with Warren Weir completing the all-Jamaican podium

Water Polo

Maggie Steffens carves her name into Olympic history with a five-goal performance to lift **USA** to a gold medal, beating Spain 8-5 in the final of the women's tournament at the Water Polo Arena

Day 13, 9 August

Who won the medals today

Morning
Canoe Sprint
Canoe Double (C2) 1000m
- Peter Kretschmer/
  Kurt Kuschela (GER) 3:33.804
- Andrei Bahdanovich/
  Aliaksandr Bahdanovich (BLR)....3:35.206
- Alexey Korovashkov/
  Ilya Pervukhin (RUS) 3:36.414

Morning
Canoe Sprint
Kayak Four (K4) 1000m
- Australia 2:55.085
- Hungary 2:55.699
- Czech Republic........................2:55.850

Morning
Canoe Sprint
Kayak Single (K1) 500m
- Danuta Kozak (HUN) 1:51.456
- Inna Osypenko-Radomska (UKR)1:52.685
- Bridgitte Hartley (RSA)...............1:52.923

Morning
Canoe Sprint
Kayak Double (K2) 500m
- Franziska Weber/
  Tina Dietze (GER).......................1:42.213
- Katalin Kovacs/
  Natasa Douchev-Janics (HUN) ...1:43.278
- Karolina Naja/
  Beata Mikolajczyk (POL) 1:44.000

Afternoon
Swimming
Women's 10km Marathon Swim
- Eva Risztov (HUN) 1:57:38.2
- Haley Anderson (USA) 1:57:38.6
- Martina Grimaldi (ITA) 1:57:41.8

Afternoon
Equestrian
Dressage Individual Competition
- Charlotte Dujardin (GBR) 90.089
- Adelinde Cornelissen (NED)..........88.196
- Laura Bechtolsheimer (GBR) 84.339

Afternoon
Boxing
Women's Fly Weight (51kg)
- Nicola Adams (GBR)..........................16
- Cancan Ren (CHN) 7
- Chungneijang Mery Kom Hmangte (IND)..
- Marlen Esparza (USA)...........................

Afternoon
Boxing
Women's Light Weight (60kg)
- Katie Taylor (IRL) 10
- Sofya Ochigava (RUS)...........................8
- Mavzuna Chorieva (TJK).........................
- Adriana Araujo (BRA) ....

Afternoon
Boxing
Women's Middle Weight (75kg)
- Claressa Shields (USA) 19
- Nadezda Torlopova (RUS) 12
- Jinzi Li (CHN) ....
- Marina Volnova (KAZ) ....

Evening
Wrestling
Women's Freestyle 55kg
- Saori Yoshida (JPN) 3
- Tonya Lynn Verbeek (CAN) 0
- Jackeline Renteria Castillo (COL) 3-1
- Yuliya Ratkevich (AZE) 3-1

Evening
Wrestling
Women's Freestyle 72kg
- Natalia Vorobieva (RUS)..........................5
- Stanka Zlateva Hristova (BUL) 0
- Guzel Manyurova (KAZ)......................3-1
- Maider Unda (ESP) 3-0

Evening
Athletics
Men's 800m
- David Lekuta Rudisha (KEN) 1:40.91 (WR)
- Nijel Amos (BOT)......................1:41.73
- Timothy Kitum (KEN)...................1:42.53

Evening
Diving
Women's 10m Platform
- Ruolin Chen (CHN) 422.30
- Brittany Broben (AUS)...................366.50
- Pandelela Rinong Pamg (MAS)......359.20

Evening
Athletics
Men's Triple Jump
- Christian Taylor (USA) 17.81m
- Will Claye (USA) 17.62m
- Fabrizio Donato (ITA) 17.48m

Evening
Athletics
Men's 200m
- Usain Bolt (JAM) 19.32
- Yohan Blake (JAM) 19.44
- Warren Weir (JAM) 19.84

Evening
Water Polo
Women's Tournament
- USA 8
- Spain..5
- Australia 13-11

Evening
Football
Women's Tournament
- USA 2
- Japan 1
- Canada 1-0

Evening
Athletics
Men's Decathlon
- Ashton Eaton (USA) 8869
- Trey Hardee (USA) 8671
- Leonel Suarez (CUB) 8523

Evening
Beach Volleyball
Men's Tournament
- Germany...2
- Brazil...1
- Latvia 2-1

Evening
Athletics
Women's Javelin
- Barbora Spotakova (CZE) 69.55m
- Christina Obergfoll (GER) 65.16m
- Linda Stahl (GER) 64.91m

Evening
Taekwondo
Women's -57kg
- Jade Jones (GBR) 6
- Yuzhuo Hou (CHN) 4
- Marlene Harnois (FRA) 12-8
- Li-Cheng Tseng (TPE) 14-2

Evening
Taekwondo
Men's -68kg
- Servet Tazegul (TUR) 6
- Mohammad Bagheri Motamed (IRI) 5
- Terrence Jennings (USA) 8-5
- Rohullah Nikpah (AFG) 5-3

USA avenge their 2011 World Cup final defeat by beating Japan in the final of the women['s] Football competition. The 2-1 v[ictory] gives USA their fourth gold me[dal] in five Olympic Games

1:43.77

Andrew Osagie finishes last (8th) in the men's 800m final, in a personal best time that would have won gold at the past three Olympic Games

100

Charlotte Dujardin (gold) and Laura Bechtolsheimer (bronze) win Great Britain its first ever medals in the 100-year history of the Dressage Individual Competition in the Olympic Games

Jade Jones fights her way to Great Britain's first Olympic Taekwondo gold medal, in the women's -57kg category at ExCeL

766

Miles of fabric used for the Games Maker uniforms — about the distance from London to Madrid

Nicola Adams' 10-month-old Doberman, Dexter watches her gold medal fight on TV in his kennel

USA's **Ashton Eaton** wins the men's Decathlon with the second highest total (8,869) at an Olympic Games. Trey Hardee's silver gives USA their first one-two in the event since 1956

Germany's Julius Brink and Jonas Reckermann shock Brazil's top seeds to win the men's Beach Volleyball gold

Medal table

17 years and 145 days

Claressa Shields (USA) becomes the second youngest Boxing gold medallist, after John Fields (USA) won the men's Feather Weight in 1924

		G	S	B	Total
1	USA	39	25	26	90
2	China	37	24	19	80
3	Great Britain	25	13	14	52
4	Russian Federation	12	21	23	56
5	Korea	12	7	6	25
6	Germany	10	16	11	37
7	France	8	9	12	29
8	Hungary	8	4	3	15
9	Italy	7	6	6	19
10	Australia	6	13	10	29
11	Kazakhstan	6	0	3	9
12	Japan	5	14	14	33
13	Netherlands	5	5	6	16
14	Islamic Republic of Iran	4	4	1	9
15	DPR Korea	4	0	1	5
16	Belarus	3	3	4	10
17	Jamaica	3	3	3	9
18	Cuba	3	3	2	8
19	New Zealand	3	2	5	10
20	Ukraine	3	1	6	10
21	South Africa	3	1	1	5
22	Spain	2	7	2	11
23	Romania	2	5	2	9
24	Denmark	2	4	3	9
25	Czech Republic	2	3	3	8
26	Brazil	2	2	7	11
27	Kenya	2	2	3	7
28	Poland	2	1	6	9
29	Croatia	2	1	1	4
30	Switzerland	2	1	0	3
31	Ethiopia	2	0	2	4
32	Canada	1	5	10	16
33	Sweden	1	3	3	7
34	Slovenia	1	1	2	4
35	Georgia	1	1	1	3
35	Norway	1	1	1	3
37	Dominican Republic	1	1	0	2
38	Ireland	1	0	1	2
38	Lithuania	1	0	1	2
38	Turkey	1	0	1	2
41	Algeria	1	0	0	1
41	Grenada	1	0	0	1
41	Venezuela	1	0	0	1
44	Colombia	0	3	3	6
45	Mexico	0	3	2	5
46	Azerbaijan	0	2	3	5
47	Egypt	0	2	0	2
48	India	0	1	3	4
48	Slovakia	0	1	3	4
50	Armenia	0	1	2	3
50	Belgium	0	1	2	3
50	Mongolia	0	1	2	3
53	Estonia	0	1	1	2
53	Indonesia	0	1	1	2
53	Malaysia	0	1	1	2
53	Serbia	0	1	1	2
53	Thailand	0	1	1	2
53	Taipei (Chinese Taipei)	0	1	1	2
53	Tunisia	0	1	1	2
60	Botswana	0	1	0	1
60	Bulgaria	0	1	0	1
60	Cyprus	0	1	0	1
60	Finland	0	1	0	1
60	Guatemala	0	1	0	1
60	Portugal	0	1	0	1
66	Greece	0	0	2	2
66	Republic of Moldova	0	0	2	2
66	Qatar	0	0	2	2
66	Singapore	0	0	2	2
70	Afghanistan	0	0	1	1
70	Argentina	0	0	1	1
70	Hong Kong, China	0	0	1	1
70	Saudi Arabia	0	0	1	1
70	Kuwait	0	0	1	1
70	Latvia	0	0	1	1
70	Morocco	0	0	1	1
70	Puerto Rico	0	0	1	1
70	Tajikistan	0	0	1	1
70	Trinidad and Tobago	0	0	1	1
70	Uzbekistan	0	0	1	1

The quartet of Tianna Madison, Allyson Felix, Bianca Knight and Carmelita Jeter create history on the track as the USA puts on a stunning display in the women's 4 x 100m Relay final. Smooth changeovers and world-class sprinting produce a new world record of 40.82sec.

In the 4 x 400m Relay, the Bahamas win their first men's Olympic gold medal in any sport, while Renaud Lavillenie of France breaks the Olympic record to win the men's Pole Vault with 5.97m.

Meanwhile, Netherlands become the second team to retain gold in the women's Hockey, beating Argentina 2-0. Earlier, Great Britain had won bronze, beating New Zealand 3-1.

And there's joy for Team GB as Lutalo Muhammad wins bronze in the Taekwondo -80kg class.

Day 14

Carmelita Jeter (right) takes the baton from Bianca Knight and powers towards the finish of the women's 4 x 100m Relay final

Boxing

Britain's Bantam Weight **Luke Campbell**, Welter Weight **Fred Evans** and Super Heavy Weight **Anthony Joshua** win semi-finals to earn a crack at gold

Cycling – BMX

Mariana Pajol becomes the second athlete from **Colombia** to win a gold medal in the Olympic Games when she wins the women's title. Sarah Walker (New Zealand) and Laura Smulders (Netherlands) take silver and bronze

Basketball

The **USA** ease into their 15th men's Basketball final at the Olympic Games with a decisive 109-83 defeat of **Argentina** at the North Greenwich Arena

Russian Federation once again dominate the Synchronised Swimming events as they take the gold in the Teams event to sweep the London 2012 Olympic titles. China and Spain take silver and bronze

Tunisia's Oussama Mellouli – also the 1500m Freestyle bronze medallist at London 2012 – wins the 10km Marathon Swim

Quote of the day

'The last 400 metres, I basically went through hell and came back to life'

Men's 10km Marathon Swim gold medallist Oussama Mellouli (TUN) reveals the agony before the ecstasy of winning at the Serpentine in Hyde Park

Ethiopian **Meseret Defar** becomes the first woman to regain the Olympic 5000m title, denying her compatriot **Tirunesh Dibaba** a successive 5000m and 10,000m Olympic Games double

Team GB's **Hannah Mills** and **Saskia Clark** win silver in the women's 470 class. They start the Medal Race on equal points with the New Zealand boat but the Kiwis prove stronger

In the -80kg class, British Taekwondo hope Lutalo Muhammad battles on to the repechage round and ultimately wins the bronze medal

The 4 x 400m Relay quartet of Chris Brown, Demetrius Pinder, Michael Mathieu and Ramon Miller win the Bahamas' first Olympic Games gold

Maris Strombergs of Latvia (left) is on his way to a successful defence of his men's Cycling – BMX title. Liam Phillips, the British challenger, crashes out

★
Star of the day
Tatyana Lysenko

Winning the World Championship title last year, Russian Federation's Tatyana Lysenko comes into London 2012 with high hopes. Lysenko breaks the Olympic record with her first throw of the final (77.56m). She then extends her lead – and the record – with a final throw of 78.18m and becomes the first reigning world champion to win the Olympic title.

Athletics

Turkey's **Asli Cakir Alptekin**, the European champion, wins the women's 1500m with compatriot Gamze Bulut taking silver. Two-time world champion Maryam Jamal (Bahrain) finishes third

Taekwondo

Korea's **Kyung-Seon Hwang** claims Olympic gold with an emphatic victory over European champion **Nur Tatar** of Turkey in the -67kg Olympic final

Day 14, 10 August

Who won the medals today

Afternoon
Sailing
Men's 470
- Mathew Belcher/Malcolm Page (AUS)...22
- Stuart Bithell/Luke Patience (GBR).........30
- Lucas Calabrese/
  Juan de la Fuente (ARG) 63

Afternoon
Sailing
Women's 470
- Jo Aleh/Olivia Powrie (NZL) 35
- Saskia Clark/Hannah Mills (GBR) 51
- Lobke Berkhout/Lisa Westerhof (NED)...64

Afternoon
Swimming
Men's 10km Marathon Swim
- Oussama Mellouli (TUN) 1:49:55.1
- Thomas Lurz (GER) 1:49:58.5
- Richard Weinberger (CAN) 1:50:00.3

Afternoon
Synchronised Swimming
Teams
- Russian Federation 197.030
- China 194.010
- Spain..193.120

Afternoon
Cycling – BMX
Women's
- Mariana Pajon (COL) 37.706
- Sarah Walker (NZL) 38.133
- Laura Smulders (NED) 38.231

Afternoon
Cycling – BMX
Men's
- Maris Strombergs (LAT) 37.576
- Sam Willoughby (AUS)................. 37.929
- Carlos Mario
  Oquendo Zabala (COL)................ 38.251

Afternoon
Wrestling
Men's Freestyle 55kg
- Dzhamal Otarsultanov (RUS) 3
- Vladimer Khinchegashvili (GEO) 1
- Shinichi Yumoto (JPN)........................3-1
- Kyong Il Yang (PRK)...........................3-1

Evening
Wrestling
Men's Freestyle 74kg
- Jordan Ernest Burroughs (USA) 3
- Sadegh Saeed Goudarzi (IRI) 0
- Soslan Tigiev (UZB) 3-0
- Denis Tsargush (RUS) 3-0

Evening
Athletics
Women's 5000m
- Meseret Defar (ETH) 15:04.25
- Vivian Jepkemoi Cheruiyot (KEN) 15:04.73
- Tirunesh Dibaba (ETH) 15:05.15

Evening
Athletics
Women's Hammer Throw
- Tatyana Lysenko (RUS) ....78.18 (OR)
- Anita Wlodarczyk (POL) 77.60
- Betty Heidler (GER) 77.12

Evening
Athletics
Women's 4 x 100m Relay
- United States .... 40.82 (WR)
- Jamaica 41.41
- Ukraine 42.04

Evening
Athletics
Women's 1500m
- Asli Cakir Alptekin (TUR).............. 4:10.23
- Gamze Bulut (TUR) 4:10.40
- Maryam Yusuf Jamal (BRN) 4:10.74

Evening
Athletics
Men's 4 x 400m Relay
- Bahamas 2:56.72
- USA 2:57.05
- Trinidad & Tobago 2:59.40

Evening
Athletics
Men's Pole Vault
- Renaud Lavillenie (FRA) .... 5.97m (OR)
- Bjorn Otto (GER) 5.91m
- Raphael Holzdeppe (GER) 5.91m

Evening
Hockey
Women's Tournament
- Netherlands 2
- Argentina..0
- Great Britain 1-3

Evening
Taekwondo
Women's -67kg
- Kyung Seon Hwang (KOR) 12
- Nur Tatar (TUR)...................................5
- Paige Mcpherson (USA).....................3-8
- Helena Fromm (GER) 8-2

Evening
Taekwondo
Men's -80kg
- Sebastian Eduardo Crismanich (ARG) 1
- Nicolas Garcia Hemme (ESP)................0
- Lutalo Muhammad (GBR) 3-9
- Mauro Sarmiento (ITA) 0-4

Great Britain win their first medal at an Olympic women's Hockey tournament for 20 years by winning their bronze medal match 3-1 against New Zealand

Grover and Elmo from TV show *Sesame Street* make it to Stratford

1952

The last Olympic Games (Helsinki) in which the USA has entered a team in the 4 x 400m Relay and failed to win

USA's Jordan Burroughs cements his rapid rise to the top of 74kg Freestyle Wrestling by taking gold

Defending champions **Netherlands** win women's Hockey gold for the third time in their history, while Great Britain secure bronze with a 3-1 win over New Zealand

4

Argentina's Luciana Aymar becomes the first female Hockey player to collect four Olympic medals. Unfortunately, none of them are gold (two silvers and two bronzes)

Medal table

1	USA	41	26	27	94
2	China	37	25	19	81
3	Great Britain	25	15	17	57
4	Russian Federation	15	21	27	63
5	Korea	13	7	7	27
6	Germany	10	18	14	42
7	France	9	9	12	30
8	Hungary	8	4	3	15
9	Australia	7	14	10	31
10	Italy	7	6	8	21
11	Netherlands	6	5	8	19
12	Kazakhstan	6	0	4	10
13	Japan	5	14	16	35
14	Islamic Republic of Iran	4	5	1	10
15	New Zealand	4	3	5	12
16	DPR Korea	4	0	2	6
17	Jamaica	3	4	3	10
18	Belarus	3	3	4	10
18	Cuba	3	3	4	10
20	Ukraine	3	1	9	13
21	South Africa	3	1	1	5
22	Ethiopia	3	0	3	6
23	Spain	2	8	3	13
24	Romania	2	5	2	9
25	Denmark	2	4	3	9
26	Czech Republic	2	3	3	8
26	Kenya	2	3	3	8
28	Brazil	2	2	8	12
29	Poland	2	2	6	10
30	Turkey	2	2	1	5
31	Croatia	2	1	1	4
32	Switzerland	2	1	0	3
33	Canada	1	5	11	17
34	Colombia	1	3	4	8
35	Sweden	1	3	3	7
36	Georgia	1	2	1	4
37	Argentina	1	1	2	4
37	Slovenia	1	1	2	4
39	Norway	1	1	1	3
39	Tunisia	1	1	1	3
41	Dominican Republic	1	1	0	2
42	Ireland	1	0	3	4
43	Lithuania	1	0	2	3
44	Latvia	1	0	1	2
45	Algeria	1	0	0	1
45	Bahamas	1	0	0	1
45	Grenada	1	0	0	1
45	Venezuela	1	0	0	1
49	Mexico	0	3	2	5
50	Azerbaijan	0	2	5	7
51	Egypt	0	2	0	2
52	India	0	1	3	4
52	Mongolia	0	1	3	4
52	Slovakia	0	1	3	4
55	Armenia	0	1	2	3
55	Belgium	0	1	2	3
57	Bulgaria	0	1	1	2
57	Estonia	0	1	1	2
57	Indonesia	0	1	1	2
57	Malaysia	0	1	1	2
57	Serbia	0	1	1	2
57	Thailand	0	1	1	2
57	Taipei (Chinese Taipei)	0	1	1	2
64	Botswana	0	1	0	1
64	Cyprus	0	1	0	1
64	Finland	0	1	0	1
64	Guatemala	0	1	0	1
64	Portugal	0	1	0	1
69	Uzbekistan	0	0	3	3
70	Greece	0	0	2	2
70	Republic of Moldova	0	0	2	2
70	Qatar	0	0	2	2
70	Singapore	0	0	2	2
70	Trinidad and Tobago	0	0	2	2
75	Afghanistan	0	0	1	1
75	Bahrain	0	0	1	1
75	Hong Kong, China	0	0	1	1
75	Saudi Arabia	0	0	1	1
75	Kuwait	0	0	1	1
75	Morocco	0	0	1	1
75	Puerto Rico	0	0	1	1
75	Tajikistan	0	0	1	1

In Sailing, Britain's men's 470 Medal Race pair Luke Patience and Stuart Bithell win silver after just failing to get the edge over the Australians Malcolm Page and Mat Belcher

Day 15

Mo at the double

There are concerns that Mo Farah might be too tired to repeat his heroics of 'Super Saturday'. Yet the 29-year-old Briton shrugs off his 10,000m exertions to win a perfectly judged 5000m and seal his position in the pantheon of Olympic distance runners.

The final night of Athletics at the Olympic Games also features Usain Bolt. Despite a strong challenge from USA's quartet, the Jamaican men's 4 x 100m Relay squad storm to gold in a new world record: 36.84sec. Bolt thus completes a historic sprint triple at consecutive Games.

Elsewhere, there are other gold medals for Team GB: Bantam Weight boxer Luke Campbell tops a day that begins with a triumph for Ed McKeever in the men's Kayak Single (K1) 200m.

Mo Farah and Usain Bolt celebrate an amazing night, having been roared to historic golds by a fervent 80,000 crowd. Here they are joined by Farah's stepdaughter

Hockey

Germany retain their men's title with a 2-1 defeat of rivals Netherlands. Two goals from Jan Philipp Rabente secures their victory

Athletics

Mariya Savinova of the Russian Federation adds the 800m title to her world crown. Hers is a high-class performance and she wins in 1:56.19. A late burst by former world champion Caster Semenya of South Africa sees her take silver

Gymnastics – Rhythmic

Russian Federation's **Evgeniya Kanaeva** becomes the first rhythmic gymnast to win two Individual All-Around Competition gold medals. She defends her title with aplomb, securing the top spot before her closest competitor has competed in the final round

Bantam Weight Luke Campbell wins Great Britain's second Boxing gold medal of the Games with a 14-11 defeat of Ireland's John Joe Nevin

Mexico shock Brazil 2-1 to win the men's Football tournament and deny the five-time World Cup winners their first Olympic gold medal

★
Star of the day
Tom Daley

A tense Aquatics Centre awaits Tom Daley. Flash photography puts him off his first dive but he is allowed a re-dive and scores 91.80. Going into the final round, he leads by 0.15. Rivals David Boudia (USA) and Bo Qiu (CHN) achieve three-figure marks with their higher-tariff dives to overtake the 18-year-old Briton but Daley's 90.75 dive is sufficient to secure bronze. He and his support team jump into the pool in celebration, whereas Qui is dejected at missing gold.

London

Quote of the day

'I wasn't going home ugly without a medal'

Australia's Jennifer Screen on beating Russian Federation in the women's Basketball bronze medal match

Wrestling

Uzbekistan's greatest Olympian **Artur Taymazov** again makes his country proud by clinching a third consecutive men's Freestyle 120kg title

Athletics

World champion **Anna Chicherova** of Russian Federation wins the women's High Jump thanks to a 2.05m clearance

Volleyball

Brazil make it two women's golds in a row by beating USA 3-1. Japan claim the bronze medal with a 3-0 victory over Korea

After scraping into the semi-final, Britain's diving darling Tom Daley improves markedly in the men's 10m Platform final to secure the bronze medal behind USA's David Boudia (gold) and China's Bo Qui (silver)

Athletics

Allyson Felix wins her third gold medal of the Olympic Games as she helps the USA quartet to a dominant victory in the 4 x 400m Relay. Felix adds this gold to her 200m and 4 x 100m Relay titles

Sailing

Spain beats Australia 3-2 to win the women's Match Racing at Weymouth and Portland. Finland take bronze, but not before an appeal from the Russians over accusations of a false start is overturned

Athletics

In a first for his nation, and the Caribbean, Trinidad and Tobago's **Keshorn Walcott** claims Javelin Throw gold with a national record of 84.58m

Day 15, 11 August

Who won the medals today

Morning
Canoe Sprint
Men's Kayak Single (K1) 200m
- Ed McKeever (GBR) 36.246
- Saul Craviotto Rivero (ESP)...........36.540
- Mark de Jonge (CAN) 36.657

Morning
Canoe Sprint
Men's Canoe Single (C1) 200m
- Yuri Cheban (UKR) 42.291
- Jevgenij Shuklin (LTU) 42.792
- Ivan Shtyl' (RUS) 42.853

Morning
Canoe Sprint
Women's Kayak Single (K1) 200m
- Lisa Carrington (NZL) 44.638
- Inna Osypenko-Radomska (UKR) ...45.053
- Natasa Douchev-Janics (HUN) 45.128

Morning
Canoe Sprint
Men's Kayak Double (K2) 200m
- Yury Postrigay/ Alexander Dyachenko (RUS).............33.507
- Raman Piatrushenka/ Vadzim Makhneu (BLR)..............34.266
- Liam Heath/Jon Schofield (GBR)....34.421

Afternoon
Athletics
Men's 50km Race Walk
- Sergey Kirdyapkin (RUS)..............3:35:59
- Jared Tallent (AUS).....................3:36:53
- Tianfeng Si (CHN) 3:37:16

Afternoon
Cycling – Mountain Bike
Women's Cross-Country
- Julie Bresset (FRA) 1:30:52
- Sabine Spitz (GER).......................1:31:54
- Georgia Gould (USA)..................1:32:00

Afternoon
Gymnastics – Rhythmic
Individual All-Around Competition
- Evgeniya Kanaeva (RUS) 116.900
- Daria Dmitrieva (RUS)................ 114.500
- Liubou Charkashyna (BLR)............111.700

Afternoon
Football
Men's Tournament
- Mexico 2
- Brazil...1
- Korea 2-0

Afternoon
Sailing
Women's Match Racing (Elliott 6m)
- Spain 3
- Australia 2
- Finland 3-1

Afternoon
Athletics
Women's 20km Race Walk
- Elena Lashmanova (RUS)..............1:25:02
- Olga Kaniskina (RUS) 1:25:09
- Shenjie Qieyang (CHN) 1:25:16

Afternoon
Wrestling
Men's Freestyle 60kg
- Toghrul Asgarov (AZE) 3
- Besik Kudukhov (RUS)...........................0
- Scott Coleman (USA) 3-1
- Yogeshwar Dutt (IND)........................3-1

Evening
Modern Pentathlon
Men's Individual Competition
- David Svoboda (CZE).....................5928
- Zhongrong Cao (CHN)...................5904
- Adam Marosi (HUN) 5836

Evening
Wrestling
Men's Freestyle 84kg
- Sharif Sharifov (AZE)...........................3
- Jaime Yusept Espinal (PUR)....................1
- Dato Marsagishvili (GEO)..................3-1
- Ehsan Naser Lashgari (IRI) 3-1

Evening
Athletics
Men's 5000m
- Mo Farah (GBR) 13:41.66
- Dejen Gebremeskel (ETH) 13:41.98
- Thomas Pkemei Longosiwa (KEN) 13:42.36

Evening
Volleyball
Women's Tournament
- Brazil 3
- USA 1
- Japan 3-0

Evening
Athletics
Women's 800m
- Mariya Savinova (RUS) 1:56.19
- Caster Semenya (RSA)..................1:57.23
- Ekaterina Poistogova (RUS) 1:57.53

Evening
Wrestling
Men's Freestyle 120kg
- Artur Taymazov (UZB) 3
- Davit Modzmanashvili (GEO)................0
- Komeil Ghasemi (IRI) 3-1
- Bilyal Makhov (RUS)........................3-1

Evening
Athletics
Women's 4 x 400m Relay
- USA....................................3:16.87
- Russian Federation 3:20.23
- Jamaica 3:20.95

Evening
Athletics
Men's Javelin Throw
- Keshorn Walcott (TRI) 84.58
- Oleksandr Pyatnytsya (UKR)...........84.51
- Antti Ruuskanen (FIN) 84.12

Evening
Boxing
Men's Light Fly Weight (49kg)
- Shiming Zou (CHN)...........................13
- Kaeo Pongprayoon (THA) 10
- Paddy Barnes (IRL) 15-15
- David Ayrapetyan (RUS) 12-13

Evening
Boxing
Men's Bantam Weight (56kg)
- Luke Campbell (GBR)......................... 14
- John Joe Nevin (IRL) 11
- Satoshi Shimizu (JPN) 11-20
- Lazaro Alvarez Estrada (CUB) 14-19

Evening
Athletics
Men's 4 x 100m Relay
- Jamaica .... 36.84 (WR)
- USA 37.04
- Trinidad and Tobago..................... 38.12

Evening
Athletics
Women's High Jump
- Anna Chicherova (RUS) 2.05
- Brigetta Barrett (USA) 2.03
- Svetlana Shkolina (RUS)..................2.03

Evening
Boxing
Men's Light Welter Weight (64kg)
- Roniel Iglesias Sotolongo (CUB) 22
- Denys Berinchyk (UKR) 15
- Vincenzo Mangiacapre (ITA)............. 8-15
- Munkh-Erdene Uranchimeg (MGL) ... 21-29

Evening
Diving
Men's 10m Platform
- David Boudia (USA) 568.65
- Bo Qiu (CHN) 566.85
- Tom Daley (GBR)...........................556.95

Evening
Hockey
Men's Tournament
- Germany..2
- Netherlands 1
- Australia 3-1

Evening
Boxing
Men's Middle Weight (75kg)
- Ryota Murata (JPN) 14
- Esquiva Falcao Florentino (BRA) 13
- Anthony Ogogo (GBR) 9-16
- Abbos Atoev (UZB) 12-13

Evening
Handball
Women's Tournament
- Norway 26
- Montenegro 23
- Spain...31-29

Evening
Boxing
Men's Heavy Weight (91kg)
- Oleksandr Usyk (UKR) 14
- Clemente Russo (ITA) 11
- Tervel Pulev (BUL) 5-21
- Teymur Mammadov (AZE)............... 13-15

Evening
Taekwondo
Women's +67kg
- Milica Mandic (SRB) 9
- Anne-Caroline Graffe (FRA) 7
- Anastasia Baryshnikova (RUS) 7-6
- Maria del Rosario Espinoza (MEX) 4-2

Evening
Taekwondo
Men's +80kg
- Carlo Molfetta (ITA) .... 9 (SUP)
- Anthony Obame (GAB) 9
- Robelis Despaigne (CUB) .... WDR
- Xiaobo Liu (CHN) 3-2

Evening
Basketball
Women's Tournament
- USA...86
- France 50
- Australia 83-74

Britain's answer to Usain Bolt on the water, accountant Ed McKeever, powers to Kayak Single (K1) 200m gold in 36.246

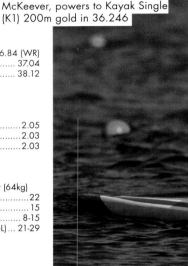

36

40mph

Diving from the 10m Platform, Olympic divers can hit the water at 40mph

Keshorn Walcott's win in the men's Javelin Throw gives Trinidad and Tobago their second gold medal, their first since Hasely Crawford's 100m win in 1976, 36 years ago

The **United States** overwhelm France in women's Basketball to win their fifth consecutive Olympic title, winning 86-50 at North Greenwich Arena

Russian **Sergey Kirdyapkin** takes gold and sets a new Olympic record in the men's 50km Race Walk with a time of 3:35:59

Usain Bolt claims his third gold in style, with a world record in the 4 x 100m Relay alongside his Jamaican team-mates

18

Mexico's victory in the final of the men's Football tournament makes them the 18th different country to win gold

5

Brazil become the first side to win five medals in the men's Football tournament at the Olympic Games without winning gold, following their 2-1 defeat by Mexico

Elena Lashmanova (RUS) becomes the youngest winner of the women's 20km Race Walk at an Olympic Games

Julie Bresset lands France's tenth gold medal of London 2012 with a dominant victory in the women's Mountain Bike race

Medal table
20 years and 124 days

		Gold	Silver	Bronze	Total
1	USA	44	29	29	102
2	China	38	27	22	87
3	Great Britain	28	15	19	62
4	Russian Federation	21	25	32	78
5	Korea	13	7	7	27
6	Germany	11	19	14	44
7	France	10	11	12	33
8	Italy	8	7	8	23
9	Hungary	8	4	5	17
10	Australia	7	16	12	35
11	Japan	6	14	17	37
12	Netherlands	6	6	8	20
13	Kazakhstan	6	0	4	10
14	Ukraine	5	4	9	18
15	New Zealand	5	3	5	13
16	Islamic Republic of Iran	4	5	3	12
17	Jamaica	4	4	4	12
18	Cuba	4	3	5	12
19	DPR Korea	4	0	2	6
20	Spain	3	9	4	16
21	Brazil	3	4	8	15
22	Belarus	3	4	5	12
23	Czech Republic	3	3	3	9
24	South Africa	3	2	1	6
25	Ethiopia	3	1	3	7
26	Romania	2	5	2	9
27	Denmark	2	4	3	9
28	Kenya	2	3	4	9
29	Poland	2	2	6	10
30	Azerbaijan	2	2	5	9
31	Turkey	2	2	1	5
32	Croatia	2	1	1	4
32	Norway	2	1	1	4
34	Switzerland	2	1	0	3
35	Canada	1	5	12	18
36	Colombia	1	3	4	8
37	Mexico	1	3	3	7
38	Sweden	1	3	3	7
39	Georgia	1	3	2	6
40	Ireland	1	1	3	5
41	Argentina	1	1	2	4
41	Lithuania	1	1	2	4
41	Slovenia	1	1	2	4
44	Serbia	1	1	1	3
44	Tunisia	1	1	1	3
46	Dominican Republic	1	1	0	2
47	Trinidad and Tobago	1	0	3	4
47	Uzbekistan	1	0	3	4
49	Latvia	1	0	1	2
50	Algeria	1	0	0	1
50	Bahamas	1	0	0	1
50	Grenada	1	0	0	1
50	Venezuela	1	0	0	1
54	Thailand	0	2	1	3
55	Egypt	0	2	0	2
56	India	0	1	4	5
57	Mongolia	0	1	3	4
57	Slovakia	0	1	3	4
59	Armenia	0	1	2	3
59	Belgium	0	1	2	3
59	Finland	0	1	2	3
62	Bulgaria	0	1	1	2
62	Estonia	0	1	1	2
62	Indonesia	0	1	1	2
62	Malaysia	0	1	1	2
62	Puerto Rico	0	1	1	2
62	Taipei (Chinese Taipei)	0	1	1	2
68	Botswana	0	1	0	1
68	Cyprus	0	1	0	1
68	Gabon	0	1	0	1
68	Guatemala	0	1	0	1
68	Montenegro	0	1	0	1
68	Portugal	0	1	0	1
74	Greece	0	0	2	2
74	Republic of Moldova	0	0	2	2
74	Qatar	0	0	2	2
74	Singapore	0	0	2	2
78	Afghanistan	0	0	1	1
78	Bahrain	0	0	1	1
78	Hong Kong, China	0	0	1	1
78	Saudi Arabia	0	0	1	1
78	Kuwait	0	0	1	1
78	Morocco	0	0	1	1
78	Tajikistan	0	0	1	1

Anthony Joshua wins
Great Britain's 29th gold
medal of the Games and
the country's third in Boxing

Day 16

Joshua lands golden blow
The London 2012 Olympic Games enters its final day, with a star-studded Closing Ceremony set to take place at the Olympic Stadium. But first, there are 15 gold medals to be handed out before the curtain comes down.

One of them goes to Britain's Anthony Joshua, who trails the defending champion Roberto Cammarelle of Italy after two rounds but rallies magnificently in the third to take a narrow decision. Team-mate Fred Evans wins a Welter Weight silver medal.

And Team GB's 65th and final medal of the Olympic Games is the silver that Samantha Murray wins in the women's Modern Pentathlon.

USA's men take their 14th Olympic Basketball title and France's also retain their crown in men's Handball with a thrilling victory over Sweden.

Boxing

Fred Evans has the chance to win Britain's 29th gold medal but Kazakhstan's Serik Sapiyev is much the stronger boxer in their 69kg Welter Weight final. Trailing after two rounds, Evans is better in the third but Sapiyev holds his own and goes on to win 17-9

Cycling — Mountain Bike

World champion **Jaroslav Kulhavy** of Czech Republic edges out Nino Schurter (SUI) on the final climb just 200m from the finish line to claim gold

Water Polo

Croatia secure their country's first Olymp Water Polo title with a 8-6 win over Italy. Pre-tournament favourites Serbia overcome Montenegro in the bronze medal match

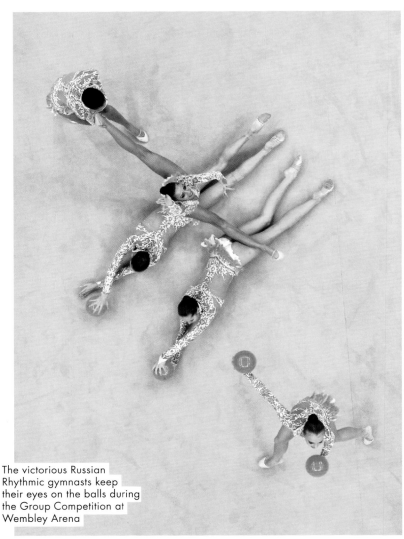

The victorious Russian Rhythmic gymnasts keep their eyes on the balls during the Group Competition at Wembley Arena

★
Star of the day

Anthony Joshua

Italian boxer Roberto Cammarelle won gold at Beijing 2008 in the Super Heavy Weight category. At the time, Anthony Joshua had not even started boxing. Now, the two meet to contest the 2012 Olympic title. Joshua gets off to a slow start, trailing 13-10 after two rounds. But he comes roaring back to tie the scores at 18-18 and win the gold on count-back.

In a rematch of the Beijing final, USA successfully defend their Olympic title with a 107-100 win over Spain. The Americans win their 14th Olympic Basketball gold, while Spain take silver for the third time – having lost to USA in each of their finals

Wrestling

Japan's **Tatsuhiro Yonemitsu** wins gold in the 66kg men's Freestyle, with Sushil Kumar of India taking silver. It is Japan's first gold medal in men's Wrestling since Seoul 1988

Volleyball

Russian Federation stage a remarkable recovery against Brazil to win gold in the men's final at Earls Court. It is the first time a country has won the title from two sets down

Quote of the day

'It is a relief because if we don't come back winners it is a disaster'

Michael D'Antoni, USA men's Basketball team assistant coach

Wrestling

Jake Stephen Varner (USA) overcomes Valerii Andriitsev of Ukraine to win the Freestyle 96kg competition. The victory gives USA multiple Olympic gold medals in the men's Wrestling competition for the first time since 1996

Modern Pentathlon

Samantha Murray wins Great Britain's 65th and last medal of these Games, in its final event, as she takes silver in the women's Modern Pentathlon. Britain have won medals in the sport at all four Olympic Games since the women's event was introduced in 2000

Day 16, 12 August

Who won the medals today

Afternoon
Athletics
Men's Marathon
- Stephen Kiprotich (UGA) 2:08:01
- Abel Kirui (KEN) 2:08:27
- Wilson Kipsang Kiprotich (KEN)... 2:09:37

Afternoon
Boxing
Men's Fly Weight (52kg)
- Robeisy Ramirez Carrazana (CUB) 17
- Tugstsogt Nyambayar (MGL) 14
- Misha Aloian (RUS) 11-15
- Michael Conlan (IRL) 10-20

Afternoon
Wrestling
Men's Freestyle 66kg
- Tatsuhiro Yonemitsu (JPN) 3
- Sushil Kumar (IND) 1
- Akzhurek Tanatarov (KAZ) 3-1
- Livan Lopez Azcuy (CUB) 5-0

Afternoon
Boxing
Men's Light Weight (60kg)
- Vasyl Lomachenko (UKR) 19
- Soon-Chul Han (KOR) 9
- Yasniel Toledo Lopez (CUB) 11-14
- Evaldas Petrauskas (LTU) 13-18

Afternoon
Volleyball
Men's Tournament
- Russian Federation 3
- Brazil 2
- Italy 3-1

Afternoon
Boxing
Men's Welter Weight (69kg)
- Serik Sapiyev (KAZ) 17
- Freddie Evans (GBR) 9
- Taras Shelestyuk (UKR) 10-11
- Andrey Zamkovoy (RUS) 12-18

Afternoon
Wrestling
Men's Freestyle 96kg
- Jacob Stephen Varner (USA) 3
- Valerii Andriitsev (UKR) 0
- George Gogshelidze (GEO) 3-1
- Khetag Gazyumov (AZE) 5-0

Afternoon
Gymnastics – Rhythmic
Group Competition
- Russian Federation 57.000
- Belarus 55.500
- Italy 55.450

Afternoon
Boxing
Men's Light Heavy Weight (81kg)
- Egor Mekhontcev (RUS) 15
- Adilbek Niyazymbetov (KAZ) 15
- Yamaguchi Falcao Florentino (BRA) ..11-23
- Oleksandr Gvozdyk (UKR) 13-13

Afternoon
Boxing
Men's Super Heavy Weight (+91kg)
- Anthony Joshua (GBR) 18
- Roberto Cammarelle (ITA) 18
- Magomedrasul Medzhidov (AZE)..... 12-13
- Ivan Dychko (KAZ) 11-13

Afternoon
Handball
Men's Tournament
- France 22
- Sweden 21
- Croatia 33-26

Afternoon
Basketball
Men's Tournament
- USA... 107
- Spain 100
- Russian Federation 81-77

Afternoon
Water Polo
Men's Tournament
- Croatia 8
- Italy 6
- Serbia 12-11

Afternoon
Modern Pentathlon
Women's
- Laura Asadauskaite (LTU) 5408
- Samantha Murray (GBR) 5356
- Yane Marques (BRA) 5340

Afternoon
Cycling – Mountain Bike
Men's Cross-Country
- Jaroslav Kulhavy (CZE) 1:29:07
- Nino Schurter (SUI) 1:29:08
- Marco Aurelio Fontana (ITA) 1:29:32

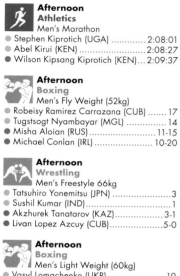

Stephen Kiprotich wins the men's Marathon on The Mall in 2:08:01, giving Uganda their second ever Olympic gold medal in Athletics

France become the first team to successfully defend the men's Handball Olympic title, beating Sweden 22-21. For the Swedes, it is the fourth time they have tasted defeat in an Olympic final

10,490
Number of athletes at the London 2012 Olympic Games

65
Great Britain surpass their medal haul at Beijing 2008 by 18, hitting a total of 65 – the biggest improvement of all countries at London 2012 compared to Beijing 2008

After three rounds, **Egor Mekontcev** (RUS) and Abilbek Niyazymbetov (KAZ) are inseparable on 15 points each. The fight goes to a count-back and the boxers are still level. The judges give their preference to decide the winner and the Russian takes gold

Medal table

302 Gold medals awarded

304 Silver medals awarded

356 Bronze medals awarded

7 Number of countries that have won a medal for the first time at London 2012: Bahrain, Botswana, Cyprus, Gabon, Grenada, Guatemala and Montenegro

85 Countries win medals at the Olympic Games

	Country	G	S	B	Total
1	USA	46	29	29	104
2	China	38	27	22	87
3	Great Britain	29	17	19	65
4	Russian Federation	24	25	33	82
5	Korea	13	8	7	28
6	Germany	11	19	14	44
7	France	11	11	12	34
8	Italy	8	9	11	28
9	Hungary	8	4	5	17
10	Australia	7	16	12	35
11	Japan	7	14	17	38
12	Kazakhstan	7	1	5	13
13	Netherlands	6	6	8	20
14	Ukraine	6	5	9	20
15	Cuba	5	3	6	14
16	New Zealand	5	3	5	13
17	Islamic Republic of Iran	4	5	3	12
18	Jamaica	4	4	4	12
19	Czech Republic	4	3	3	10
20	DPR Korea	4	0	2	6
21	Spain	3	10	4	17
22	Brazil	3	5	9	17
23	Belarus	3	5	5	13
24	South Africa	3	2	1	6
25	Ethiopia	3	1	3	7
26	Croatia	3	1	2	6
27	Romania	2	5	2	9
28	Kenya	2	4	5	11
29	Denmark	2	4	3	9
30	Azerbaijan	2	2	6	10
30	Poland	2	2	6	10
32	Turkey	2	2	1	5
33	Switzerland	2	2	0	4
34	Lithuania	2	1	2	5
35	Norway	2	1	1	4
36	Canada	1	5	12	18
37	Sweden	1	4	3	8
38	Colombia	1	3	4	8
39	Georgia	1	3	3	7
39	Mexico	1	3	3	7
41	Ireland	1	1	3	5
42	Argentina	1	1	2	4
42	Slovenia	1	1	2	4
42	Serbia	1	1	2	4
45	Tunisia	1	1	1	3
46	Dominican Republic	1	1	0	2
47	Trinidad and Tobago	1	0	3	4
47	Uzbekistan	1	0	3	4
49	Latvia	1	0	1	2
50	Algeria	1	0	0	1
50	Bahamas	1	0	0	1
50	Grenada	1	0	0	1
50	Uganda	1	0	0	1
50	Venezuela	1	0	0	1
55	India	0	2	4	6
56	Mongolia	0	2	3	5
57	Thailand	0	2	1	3
58	Egypt	0	2	0	2
59	Slovakia	0	1	3	4
60	Armenia	0	1	2	3
60	Belgium	0	1	2	3
60	Finland	0	1	2	3
63	Bulgaria	0	1	1	2
63	Estonia	0	1	1	2
63	Indonesia	0	1	1	2
63	Malaysia	0	1	1	2
63	Puerto Rico	0	1	1	2
63	Taipei (Chinese Taipei)	0	1	1	2
69	Botswana	0	1	0	1
69	Cyprus	0	1	0	1
69	Gabon	0	1	0	1
69	Guatemala	0	1	0	1
69	Montenegro	0	1	0	1
69	Portugal	0	1	0	1
75	Greece	0	0	2	2
75	Republic of Moldova	0	0	2	2
75	Qatar	0	0	2	2
75	Singapore	0	0	2	2
79	Afghanistan	0	0	1	1
79	Bahrain	0	0	1	1
79	Hong Kong, China	0	0	1	1
79	Saudi Arabia	0	0	1	1
79	Kuwait	0	0	1	1
79	Morocco	0	0	1	1
79	Tajikistan	0	0	1	1

CLASS OF 2012

The complete Team GB register of athletes who competed at the London 2012 Olympic Games

Archery

Men's

Individual Competition
Larry Godfrey.................Third round
Simon Terry.................Second round
Alan Wills....................First round

Team Competition
Larry Godfrey, Simon Terry,
Alan Wills....................First round

Women's

Individual Competition
Naomi Folkard............Second round
Amy Oliver.................Second round
Alison Williamson.............First round

Team Competition
Naomi Folkard, Amy Oliver,
Alison Williamson..........First round

Athletics

Men's

100m
Dwain Chambers ....Semi-final
James Dasaolu................Semi-final
Adam Gemili................Semi-final

200m
James Ellington................First round
Christian Malcolm.............Semi-final

400m
Nigel Levine.................Semi-final
Martyn Rooney.................Semi-final
Conrad Williams................Semi-final

800m
Andrew Osagie 8th
Michael Rimmer .... First round
Gareth Warburton .... First round

1500m
Andrew Baddeley ....Semi-final
Ross Murray ....Semi-final

5000m
Mo Farah ....
Nick McCormick............ First round

10,000m
Mo Farah ....
Chris Thompson 25th

110m Hurdles
Lawrence Clarke 4th
Andrew Pozzi .... DNF
Andy Turner ....Semi-final

400m Hurdles
Dai Greene........................... 4th
Jack Green ....Semi-final
Rhys Williams ....Semi-final

3000m Steeplechase
Stuart Stokes..................First round

4 x 100m Relay
Dwain Chambers, Adam Gemili,
Christian Malcolm,
Danny Talbot ....DSQ

4 x 400m Relay
Jack Green, Dai Greene,
Nigel Levine, Martyn Rooney,
Conrad Williams....................4th

Discus Throw
Lawrence Okoye................12th
Brett Morse ....Qualifying round
Abdul Buhari ....Qualifying round

Hammer Throw
Alex Smith....................12th

High Jump
Robbie Grabarz.....................

Javelin Throw
Mervyn Luckwell ...Qualifying round

Long Jump
Greg Rutherford ....
Chris Tomlinson 6th

Pole Vault
Steve Lewis .... =5th

Shot Put
Carl Myerscough ..Qualifying round

Triple Jump
Phillips Idowu ....Qualifying round

Decathlon
Daniel Awde .... DNF

50km Race Walk
Dominic King 51st

Marathon
Lee Merrien 30th
Scott Overall 61st

Women's

100m
Anyika Onuora .... First round
Abi Oyepitan ....Semi-final

200m
Margaret Adeoye............Semi-final
Anyika Onuora .... First round
Abi Oyepitan ....Semi-final

400m
Shana Cox ....Semi-final
Lee McConnell ....Semi-final
Christine Ohuruogu...................

800m
Lynsey Sharp ....Semi-final

1500m
Lisa Dobriskey..................... 10th
Hannah England ....Semi-final
Laura Weightman 11th

5000m
Julia Bleasdale 8th
Barbara Parker.............. First round
Jo Pavey 7th

10,000m
Julia Bleasdale 8th
Jo Pavey 7th

100m Hurdles
Tiffany Porter ....Semi-final

400m Hurdles
Perri Shakes-Drayton ....Semi-final
Eilidh Child ....Semi-final

3000m Steeplechase
Barbara Parker.............. First round
Eilish McColgan............. First round

4 x 400m Relay
Shana Cox, Eilidh Child,
Lee McConnell, Christine Ohuruogu,
Perri Shakes-Drayton 5th

Hammer Throw
Sophie Hitchon 12th

Javelin Throw
Goldie Sayers ......Qualifying round

Long Jump
Shara Proctor.........................9th

Pole Vault
Holly Bleasdale .... =6th
Kate Dennison ......Qualifying round

Triple Jump
Yamile Aldama 5th

Heptathlon
Jessica Ennis ....
Louise Hazel 27th
Katarina Johnson-Thompson 15th

20km Race Walk
Jo Jackson ....DSQ

Marathon
Claire Hallissey....................57th
Freya Murray 44th
Mara Yamauchi .... DNF

Badminton

Men's

Singles
Rajiv Ouseph...............Group stage

Women's

Singles
Susan Egelstaff............Group stage

Mixed

Doubles
Chris Adcock and
Imogen Bankier............ Group stage

Basketball

Men's

Kieron Achara, Robert Archibald, Eric
Boateng, Dan Clark, Luol Deng, Joel
Freeland, Kyle Johnson, Andrew
Lawrence, Mike Lenzly, Pops
Mensah-Bonsu, Nate Reinking,
Drew Sullivan .... Group stage

Women's

Dominique Allen, Rose Anderson, Kim
Butler, Stef Collins, Temi Fagbenle,
Chantelle Handy, Jo Leedham,
Julie Page, Natalie Stafford, Azania
Stewart, Rachael Vanderwal,
Jenaya Wade-Fray ......Group stage

Beach Volleyball

Men's

John Garcia-Thompson and
Steve Grotowski..........Group stage

Women's

Zara Dampney and
Shauna Mullin ......Lucky loser stage

Boxing

Men's

Fly Weight (52kg)
Andrew Selby.............Quarter-final

Bantam Weight (56kg)
Luke Campbell ....

Light Weight (60kg)
Josh Taylor ....Second round

Light Welter Weight (64kg)
Tom Stalker ....Quarter-final

Welter Weight (69kg)
Fred Evans ....

Middle Weight (75kg)
Anthony Ogogo ....

Super Heavy Weight (+91kg)
Anthony Joshua ....

Women's

Fly Weight (51kg)
Nicola Adams ....

Light Weight (60kg)
Natasha Jonas............Quarter-final

Middle Weight (75kg)
Savannah Marshall......Quarter-final

Canoe Slalom
Men's
Kayak Single (K1)
Richard Hounslow ....Semi-final
Canoe Single (C1)
David Florence...............Semi-final
Canoe Double (C2)
Tim Baillie and
Etienne Stott ....⊛
David Florence and
Richard Hounslow ....⊛

Women's
Kayak Single (K1)
Lizzie Neave ....Semi-final

Canoe Sprint
Men's
Kayak Single (K1) 200m
Ed McKeever.............................⊛
Kayak Double (K2) 200m
Liam Heath and
Jon Schofield ....⊛
Kayak Single (K1) 1000m
Tim Brabants..........................8th
Canoe Single (C1) 200m
Richard Jefferies ....Semi-final
Canoe Single (C1) 1000m
Richard Jefferies 15th

Women's
Kayak Single (K1) 200m
Jess Walker 7th
Kayak Single (K1) 500m
Rachel Cawthorn 6th
Kayak Double (K2) 500m
Abigail Edmonds, Louisa Sawers 11th
Kayak Four (K4) 500m
Rachel Cawthorn, Angela Hannah,
Louisa Sawers, Jess Walker 5th

Cycling — BMX
Men's
Liam Phillips...........................8th

Women's
Shanaze Reade 6th

Cycling — Mountain Bike
Men's
Liam Killeen ....DNF

Women's
Annie Last 8th

Cycling — Road
Men's
Road Race
Mark Cavendish 29th
Chris Froome 109th
David Millar...................... 108th
Ian Stannard...................... 94th
Bradley Wiggins 103rd

Women's
Road Race
Lizzie Armitstead ....⊛
Nicole Cooke 31st
Lucy Martin .... OTL
Emma Pooley..................... 40th

Men's
Time Trial
Chris Froome ....⊛
Bradley Wiggins ....⊛

Women's
Time Trial
Lizzie Armitstead 10th
Emma Pooley......................... 6th

Cycling — Track
Men's
Keirin
Sir Chris Hoy ....⊛
Omnium
Ed Clancy.............................⊛
Sprint
Jason Kenny ....⊛
Team Pursuit
Steven Burke, Ed Clancy
Peter Kennaugh, Geraint Thomas ⊛
Team Sprint
Philip Hindes, Sir Chris Hoy
Jason Kenny ....⊛

Women's
Keirin
Victoria Pendleton...................⊛
Omnium
Laura Trott ....⊛
Sprint
Victoria Pendleton...................⊛
Team Pursuit
Dani King, Joanna Rowsell,
Laura Trott ....⊛
Team Sprint
Victoria Pendleton
and Jess Varnish ....DSQ

Diving
Men's
3m Springboard
Jack Laugher.........Preliminary round
Chris Mears 9th
10m Platform
Tom Daley ....⊛
Pete Waterfield .....Preliminary round
Synchronised 3m Springboard
Chris Mears and
Nick Robinson-Baker 5th
Synchronised 10m Platform
Tom Daley and
Peter Waterfield 4th

Women's
3m Springboard
Rebecca Gallantree.........Semi-final
Hannah Starling ....Semi-final
10m Platform
Stacie Powell........Preliminary round
Monique Gladding
.......................Preliminary round
Synchronised 3m Springboard
Alicia Blagg and
Rebecca Gallantree................. 7th
Synchronised 10m Platform
Tonia Couch and Sarah Barrow 5th

Equestrian — Dressage
Mixed
Individual Competition
Laura Bechtolsheimer on
Mistral Hojris ....⊛
Richard Davison on Artemis ..... GPS
Charlotte Dujardin on Valegro....⊛
Carl Hester on Uthopia 5th
Team Competition
Laura Bechtolsheimer on
Mistral Hojris, Carl Hester on
Uthopia, Charlotte Dujardin
on Valegro ....⊛

Equestrian — Eventing
Mixed
Individual Competition
Kristina Cook on Miners Frolic ...6th
William Fox-Pitt on Lionheart 27th
Mary King on Imperial Cavalier . 5th
Zara Phillips on High Kingdom... 8th
Nicola Wilson on Opp' Buzz .. 28th
Team Competition
Kristina Cook on Miners Frolic,
William Fox-Pitt on Lionheart, Mary
King on Imperial Cavalier, Zara
Phillips on High Kingdom, Nicola
Wilson on Opposition Buzz ......⊛

Equestrian — Jumping
Mixed
Individual Competition
Scott Brash on Hello Sanctos... =5th
Peter Charles on Vindicat ...... =65th
Ben Maher on Tripple X.......... =9th
Nick Skelton on Big Star .... =5th
Team Competition
Scott Brash on Hello Sanctos, Peter
Charles on Vindicat, Ben Maher on
Tripple X, Nick Skelton on Big Star ⊛

Fencing
Men's
Individual Foil
James-Andrew Davis ..Second round
Richard Kruse ....Second round
Husayn Rosowsky........... First round
Team Foil
James-Andrew Davis, Laurence
Halsted, Richard Kruse, Husayn
Rosowsky.............................. 6th
Individual Sabre
James Honeybone .... First round

Women's
Individual Epée
Corinna Lawrence .....Second round
Individual Foil
Anna Bentley................. First round
Natalia Sheppard .....Second round
Sophie Troiano .... First round
Team Foil
Anna Bentley, Martina Emanuel,
Natalia Sheppard, Sophie Troiano 8th
Individual Sabre
Louise Bond-Williams ...... First round
Sophie Williams............. First round

Football
Men's
Joe Allen, Craig Bellamy, Ryan
Bertrand, Jack Butland, Steven Caulker,
Tom Cleverley, Jack Cork, Craig
Dawson, Ryan Giggs, Aaron Ramsey,
Micah Richards, Danny Rose, Scott
Sinclair, Marvin Sordell, Jason Steele,
Daniel Sturridge, Neil Taylor,
James Tomkins.................Quarter-final

Women's
Eniola Aluko, Anita Asante, Karen
Bardsley, Sophie Bradley, Rachel
Brown, Karen Carney, Ifeoma Dieke
(replaced by Dunia Susi), Stephanie
Houghton, Kim Little, Claire Rafferty,
Alex Scott, Jill Scott, Kelly Smith,
Casey Stoney, Fara Williams,
Rachel Williams, Ellen White,
Rachel Yankey .... Quarter-final

Gymnastics — Artistic

Men's

Individual All-Around Competition
Dan Purvis.........................13th
Kristian Thomas.................. 7th
Pommel Horse Competition
Louis Smith .... ✱
Max Whitlock .... ✱
Vault Competition
Kristian Thomas 8th
Team Competition
Sam Oldham, Dan Purvis, Louis Smith,
Kristian Thomas, Max Whitlock ...... ✱

Women's

Individual All-Around Competition
Rebecca Tunney....................13th
Hannah Whelan 24th
Uneven Bars Competition
Beth Tweddle .... ✱
Team Competition
Imogen Cairns, Jennifer Pinches,
Rebecca Tunney, Beth Tweddle,
Hannah Whelan 6th

Gymnastics — Rhythmic

Women's

Group Competition
Georgina Cassar, Jade Faulkner,
Francesca Fox, Lynne Hutchison, Louisa
Pouli, Rachel Smith .... Qualifying round
Individual All-Around Competition
Francesca Jones .... Qualifying round

Gymnastics — Trampoline

Women's

Individual Competition
Kat Driscoll...........Qualifying round

Handball

Men's

Seb Edgar, Robin Garnham, Martin
Hare, Mark Hawkins, Steven Larsson,
Chris McDermott, Dan McMillan,
Chris Mohr, Jesper Parker, John Pearce,
Seb Prieto, Gawain Vincent, Ciaran
Williams, Bobby White ... Group stage

Women's

Lyn Byl, Kelsi Fairbrother, Kathryn Fudge,
Marie Gerbron, Britt Goodwin, Sarah
Hargreaves, Nina Heglund, Louise Jukes,
Holly Lam-Moores, Yvonne Leuthold, Jane
Mayes, Lynn McCafferty, Ewa Palies,
Zoë van der Weel. ....Group stage

Hockey

Men's

Nicholas Catlin, Jonty Clarke, Matt
Daly, James Fair, Dan Fox, Ben
Hawes, Ashley Jackson, Glenn
Kirkham, Iain Lewers, Iain Mackay,
Harry Martin, Barry Middleton,
Robert Moore, Richard Smith, James
Tindall, Alastair Wilson 4th

Women's

Ashleigh Ball, Laura Bartlett,
Crista Cullen, Alex Danson,
Hannah Macleod, Emily Maguire,
Anne Panter, Helen Richardson,
Chloe Rogers, Beth Storry,
Sarah Thomas, Georgie Twigg,
Laura Unsworth, Kate Walsh,
Sally Walton, Nicola White ...... ✱

Judo

Men's

Extra Lightweight (up to 60kg)
Ashley McKenzie ......Second round
Half-Lightweight (60-66kg)
Colin Oates .... Quarter-final
Lightweight (66-73kg)
Daniel Williams ....Second round
Half-Middleweight (73-81kg)
Euan Burton..............Second round
Middleweight (81-90kg)
Winston Gordon ....Second round
Half-Heavyweight (90-100kg)
James Austin .... First round
Heavyweight (over 100kg)
Chris Sherrington........Second round

Women's

Extra Lightweight (up to 48kg)
Kelly Edwards...........Second round
Half-Lightweight (48-52kg)
Sophie Cox.................... First round
Lightweight (52-57kg)
Sarah Clark .... First round
Half-Middleweight (57-63kg)
Gemma Howell .... First round
Middleweight (63-70kg)
Sally Conway ....Second round
Half-Heavyweight (70-78kg)
Gemma Gibbons .... ✱
Heavyweight (over 78kg)
Karina Bryant......................... ✱

Modern Pentathlon

Men's

Sam Weale 13th
Nick Woodbridge................. 10th

Women's

Samantha Murray.................... ✱
Mhairi Spence 21st

Rowing

Men's

Single Sculls
Alan Campbell .... ✱
Pair
George Nash and Will Satch ... ✱
Double Sculls
Bill Lucas and Sam Townsend 5th
Lightweight Double Sculls
Mark Hunter and Zac Purchase.. ✱
Four
Alex Gregory, Tom James, Pete
Reed, Andrew Triggs Hodge ..... ✱
Lightweight Four
Chris Bartley, Peter Chambers
Richard Chambers, Rob Williams ✱
Quadruple Sculls
Charles Cousins, Stephen
Rowbotham, Tom Solesbury
Matthew Wells 5th
Eight
Richard Egington, James Foad,
Matthew Langridge,
Constantine Louloudis,
Alex Partridge, Tom Ransley,
Mohamed Sbihi, Greg Searle,
Phelan Hill (cox) .... ✱

Women's

Pair
Helen Glover and
Heather Stanning .... ✱
Double Sculls
Katherine Grainger and
Anna Watkins .... ✱
Lightweight Double Sculls
Katherine Copeland and
Sophie Hosking .... ✱
Quadruple Sculls
Debbie Flood, Frances Houghton
Beth Rodford, Melanie Wilson ... 6th
Eight
Jessica Eddie, Katie Greves,
Lindsey Maguire, Natasha Page,
Louisa Reeve, Victoria Thornley,
Annabel Vernon, Olivia Whitlam,
Caroline O'Connor (cox) 5th

Sailing

Men's

Windsurfer (RS:X)
Nick Dempsey....................... ✱
One-Person Dinghy (Laser)
Paul Goodison....................... 7th
**One-Person Dinghy
(Heavyweight) (Finn)**
Ben Ainslie........................... ✱
Two-Person Dinghy (470)
Stuart Bithell and Luke Patience .. ✱
Skiff (49er)
Stevie Morrison and Ben Rhodes 5th
Keelboat (Star)
Iain Percy and Andrew Simpson ✱

Women's

Windsurfer (RS:X)
Bryony Shaw.......................... 7th
One-Person Dinghy (Laser Radial)
Alison Young 5th
Two-Person Dinghy (470)
Saskia Clark and Hannah Mills.. ✱
Match Racing (Elliott 6m)
Annie Lush, Kate Macgregor,
Lucy Macgregor.......... Quarter-final

Shooting

Men's

50m Rifle Prone (60 Shots Prone)
Jon Hammond .... ..Qualifying round
James Huckle........Qualifying round
50m Rifle 3 Positions (3x40 Shots)
Jon Hammond .... ..Qualifying round
James Huckle........Qualifying round
10m Air Rifle (60 Shots Standing)
James Huckle........Qualifying round
Skeet (125 Targets)
Rory Warlow.........Qualifying round
Richard Brickell .....Qualifying round
Trap (125 Targets)
Ed Ling ....Qualifying round
Double Trap (150 Targets)
Richard Faulds ......Qualifying round
Peter Wilson.......................... ✱

Women's

10m Air Pistol (40 Shots)
Georgina Geikie...Qualifying round
25m Pistol (30+30 Shots)
Georgina Geikie...Qualifying round
10m Air Rifle (40 Shots)
Jennifer McIntosh...Qualifying round
Skeet
Elena Allen...........Qualifying round
Trap
Charlotte Kerwood Qualifying round

Swimming

Men's

100m Backstroke
Liam Tancock 5th
Chris Walker-Hebborn .... First round

200m Backstroke
Marco Loughran .... First round
Chris Walker-Hebborn .... First round

100m Breaststroke
Craig Benson .... Semi-final
Michael Jamieson .... Semi-final

200m Breaststroke
Michael Jamieson .... 🏅
Andrew Willis 8th

100m Butterfly
Antony James .... First round
Michael Rock .... First round

200m Butterfly
Roberto Pavoni .... First round
Joe Roebuck .... First round

50m Freestyle
Adam Brown .... First round

100m Freestyle
Adam Brown .... First round

200m Freestyle
Ieuan Lloyd .... First round
Robbie Renwick 6th

400m Freestyle
David Carry 7th
Robbie Renwick .... First round

1500m Freestyle
Dave Davies .... First round
Daniel Fogg 8th

200m Individual Medley
James Goddard 7th
Joe Roebuck .... Semi-final

400m Individual Medley
Roberto Pavoni .... First round
Joe Roebuck .... First round

4 x 100m Freestyle Relay
Simon Burnett, Grant Turner, James Disney-May, Craig Gibbons First round

4 x 200m Freestyle Relay
Rob Bale, David Carry, Ieuan Lloyd, Ross Davenport, Robbie Renwick .. 6th

4 x 100m Individual Medley Relay
Craig Benson, Adam Brown, Michael Jamieson, Michael Rock, Liam Tancock 4th

10km Marathon Swim
Daniel Fogg 5th

Women's

100m Backstroke
Georgia Davies .... Semi-final
Gemma Spofforth 5th

200m Backstroke
Steph Proud .... Semi-final
Elizabeth Simmonds 4th

100m Breaststroke
Kate Haywood .... First round
Siobhan-Marie O'Connor First round

200m Breaststroke
Stacey Tadd .... First round

100m Butterfly
Ellen Gandy 8th
Fran Halsall .... Semi-final

200m Butterfly
Ellen Gandy .... First round
Jemma Lowe 6th

50m Freestyle
Fran Halsall 5th
Amy Smith .... Semi-final

100m Freestyle
Fran Halsall 6th
Amy Smith .... Semi-final

200m Freestyle
Caitlin McClatchey 7th
Rebecca Turner .... First round

400m Freestyle
Rebecca Adlington .... 🏅
Jo Jackson .... First round

800m Freestyle
Rebecca Adlington .... 🏅
Ellie Faulkner .... First round

200m Individual Medley
Sophie Allen .... First round
Hannah Miley 7th

400m Individual Medley
Hannah Miley 5th
Aimee Willmott .... First round

4 x 100m Freestyle Relay
Fran Halsall, Jess Lloyd, Caitlin McClatchey, Rebecca Turner, Amy Smith 5th

4 x 200 Freestyle Relay
Ellie Faulkner, Jo Jackson, Caitlin McClatchey, Hannah Miley, Rebecca Turner 5th

4 x 100m Individual Medley Relay
Ellen Gandy, Fran Halsall, Jemma Lowe, Siobhan-Marie O'Connor, Amy Smith, Gemma Spofforth.... 8th

10km Marathon Swim
Keri-Anne Payne 4th

Synchronised Swimming

Women's

Duets
Olivia Federici and Jenna Randall 9th

Teams
Yvette Baker, Katie Clark, Katie Dawkins, Olivia Federici, Jennifer Knobbs, Vicki Lucass, Asha Randall, Jenna Randall, Katie Skelton 6th

Table Tennis

Men's

Singles
Paul Drinkhall .... Third round

Team
Andrew Baggaley, Paul Drinkhall, Liam Pitchford .... First round

Women's

Singles
Joanna Parker .... Second round

Team
Kelly Sibley, Na Liu, Joanna Parker .... First round

Taekwondo

Men's

-68kg
Martin Stamper .... =5th

-80kg
Lutalo Muhammad .... 🏅

Women's

-57kg
Jade Jones .... 🏅

-67kg
Sarah Stevenson .... First round

Tennis

Men's

Singles
Andy Murray .... 🏅

Doubles
Andy Murray and
Jamie Murray .... First round
Colin Fleming and
Ross Hutchins .... First round

Women's

Singles
Anne Keothavong .... First round
Elena Baltacha .... Second round
Heather Watson .... Second round
Laura Robson .... Second round

Doubles
Laura Robson and
Heather Watson .... First round
Elena Baltacha and
Anne Keothavong .... First round

Mixed

Doubles
Andy Murray and Laura Robson 🏅

Triathlon

Men's

Alistair Brownlee .... 🏅
Jonny Brownlee .... 🏅
Stuart Hayes 37th

Women's

Lucy Hall 33rd
Vicky Holland 26th
Helen Jenkins 5th

Volleyball

Men's

Dami Bakare, Peter Bakare Nathan French, Jason Haldane, Dan Hunter, Chris Lamont, Mark McGivern, Joel Miller, Kieran O'Malley, Andrew Pink, Ben Pipes, Mark Plotyczer .... Group stage

Women's

Lynne Beattie, Maria Bertelli, Rachel Bragg, Grace Carter, Rachel Laybourne, Savanah Leaf, Ciara Michel, Joanne Morgan, Lizzie Reid, Janine Sandell, Jennifer Taylor, Lucy Wicks .... Group stage

Water Polo

Men's

Craig Figes, Matt Holland, Ciaran James, Sean King, Joseph O'Regan, Rob Parker, Alex Parsonage, Glen Robinson, Sean Ryder, Adam Scholefield, Edward Scott, Jake Vincent, Jack Waller ..... Group stage

Women's

Francesca Clayton, Lisa Gibson, Ciara Gibson-Byrne, Beckie Kershaw, Fran Leighton, Fiona McCann, Rosie Morris, Hazel Musgrove. Robyn Nicholls, Francesca Painter-Snell, Alex Rutlidge, Chloe Wilcox, Angie Winstanley-Smith 8th

Weightlifting

Men's

69kg
Gareth Evans 17th

77kg
Jack Oliver 10th

94kg
Peter Kirkbride 16th

Women's

58kg
Zoe Smith 12th

69kg
Natasha Perdue 12th

Wrestling

Women's

Freestyle 55kg
Olga Butkevych .... Second round

1 Lizzie Armitstead	**13** Peter Wilson	**23** Alex Gregory
2 Rebecca Adlington	**14** Gemma Gibbons	Pete Reed
3 Dan Purvis	**15** Philip Hindes	Tom James
Max Whitlock	Jason Kenny	Andrew Triggs Hodge
Louis Smith	Sir Chris Hoy	**24** Katherine Copeland
Kristian Thomas	**16** William Satch	Sophie Hosking
Sam Oldham	George Nash	**25** Mark Hunter
4 Nicola Wilson	**17** Anna Watkins	Zac Purchase
Zara Phillips	Katherine Grainger	**26** Dani King
William Fox-Pitt	**18** Alan Campbell	Laura Trott
Mary King	**19** Karina Bryant	Joanna Rowsell
Kristina Cook	**20** Ed Clancy	**27** Jessica Ennis
5 Helen Glover	Steven Burke	**28** Greg Rutherford
Heather Stanning	Peter Kennaugh	**29** Mo Farah

6 James Foad	Geraint Thomas
Tom Ransley	**21** Victoria Pendleton
Richard Egington	**22** Rebecca Adlington
Matthew Langridge	**30** Iain Percy
Alex Partridge	Andrew Simpson
Mohamed Sbihi	**31** Ben Ainslie
Phelan Hill	**32** Louis Smith
Greg Searle	**33** Max Whitlock
Constantine Louloudis	**34** Andy Murray

7 Bradley Wiggins
8 Chris Froome
9 Michael Jamieson
10 Peter Chambers
Richard Chambers
Rob Williams
Chris Bartley
11 Etienne Stott
Tim Baillie
12 David Florence
Richard Hounslow

35 ● Ed Clancy
36 ● Laura Robson
       Andy Murray
37 ● Christine Ohuruogu
38 ● Beth Tweddle
39 ● Nick Skelton
       Ben Maher
       Scott Brash
       Peter Charles
40 ● Jason Kenny
41 ● Alistair Brownlee
42 ● Jonny Brownlee
43 ● Nick Dempsey
44 ● Carl Hester
       Laura Bechtolsheimer
       Charlotte Dujardin
45 ● Laura Trott
46 ● Victoria Pendleton
47 ● Sir Chris Hoy
48 ● Robbie Grabarz

49 ● Charlotte Dujardin
50 ● Laura Bechtolsheimer
51 ● Nicola Adams
52 ● Jade Jones
53 ● Luke Patience
       Stuart Bithell
54 ● Saskia Clark
       Hannah Mills
55 ● Anthony Ogogo

56 ● Georgie Twigg
       Emily Maguire
       Chloe Rogers
       Nicola White
       Ashleigh Ball
       Sally Walton
       Laura Unsworth
       Sarah Thomas
       Helen Richardson
       Crista Cullen
       Anne Panter
       Hannah Macleod
       Beth Storry
       Alex Danson
       Laura Bartlett
       Kate Walsh
57 ● Lutalo Muhammad
58 ● Ed McKeever
59 ● Jon Schofield
       Liam Heath

60 ● Mo Farah
61 ● Luke Campbell
62 ● Tom Daley
63 ● Fred Evans
64 ● Anthony Joshua
65 ● Samantha Murray

Team GB's final medal count

29
19   17

LASTING LEGACY

London 2012 has proven there is more to the legacy of the Olympic Games than sport

WORDS NIKKI WICKS

Some said it would be David Beckham, others were convinced it would be Sir Roger Bannister or Sir Steve Redgrave. The mystery surrounding who would light the London 2012 Olympic Cauldron was the best kept secret of Danny Boyle's spectacular Opening Ceremony. And the decision to hand over the incredible honour to seven young, hopeful British athletes, and not to use a well-known personality, was a telling statement.

To an estimated audience of around one billion people worldwide, the gesture was a clear nod to the promises made in London's bid to host the 2012 Olympic Games, some seven years earlier.

'Your decision today is critical,' said Sebastian Coe, Chair of the London Organising Committee of the Olympic Games and Paralympic Games, in his final summing up of the city's bid in 2005.

'It is a decision about which bid offers the vision and sporting legacy to best promote the Olympic cause. It is a decision about which city will help us show a new generation why sport matters.'

London was chosen as the Host City for the 2012 Games thanks largely to a promise that it would deliver a legacy. And it's a promise that's been kept. 'London has raised the bar on how to deliver a lasting legacy,' said Jacques Rogge, the International Olympic Committee President. 'This great historical city has created a legacy blueprint for future Games hosts.'

There's no better evidence of this than in the groundbreaking International

Inspiration programme – the first international sports programme ever implemented by an Olympic Host City. In its bid to host the Games, London 2012 organisers made an ambitious pledge to use sport to improve the lives of 12 million children in 20 countries (a figure inspired by the 2012 numerals), before the Games had even begun.

In July 2011, a year ahead of schedule, the project reached its goal as its various initiatives touched the lives of young people around the world, from Uganda and Tanzania to Jordon and India. In Bangladesh, the impact of the programme went beyond anyone's expectations. The initiative set out to teach young children how to swim in an attempt to help alleviate the alarming statistic that every 15 minutes a child drowns in the flood-prone country. As a result, more than 80,000 children have now learnt vital survival swimming skills and lives have been saved.

'Sport can change lives. I have seen this first hand from my work with International Inspiration,' said David Beckham.

'This has changed lives, opening doors to building confidence, better health, inclusion, excellence or simply the joy of taking part. The legacy that these Games will leave, not just here but around the world, will no doubt be a long lasting one.'

Legacy hasn't always been at the forefront of Olympic planning: at times has been an afterthought to Games organisers, where, as Rogge himself has conceded, 'some Host Cities have fared better than others.'

Having staged the greatest sporting event on earth, the Olympic Park will soon be transformed into a brand new residential area of London
(computer generated image)

But for the organisers of London 2012 legacy would be the concept that was central to its Olympic Games plans. 'Legacy is probably nine-tenths of what this process is about, not just 16 days of Olympic sport,' said Coe, back in 2006.

Now that the medals have been won and the baton passed to Rio de Janeiro, the 2016 Host City, what's next for London and the UK? At the heart of London's legacy ambition is the Olympic Park, where revitalising London's six Host Boroughs (Barking & Dagenham, Greenwich, Hackney, Newham, Tower Hamlets and Waltham Forest) was a key objective.

During the Games a once-neglected area became the centre of the world, as all eyes turned towards east London, where the world's best athletes competed for Olympic Games glory. And as the Games reach an end, the attention on the area is set to continue.

In the 18 months from October 2012, the 560-acre Olympic Park – to be renamed Queen Elizabeth Olympic Park – will be transformed. Plans include the development of the South Plaza, an area in the park's southern end between the Aquatics Centre, the Olympic Stadium and the Orbit.

Designed by the landscape architects who created the award-winning High Line in New York, the South Plaza will become a new open space, furnished with fountains, light spectaculars, garden areas and temporary installations such as urban beaches.

'There's no doubt that this is much more than an Olympic Park,' said

British designer Wayne Hemingway, following a visit to the Park. 'This is a high-quality, well thought out piece of "place making". There's clearly been a lot of thought gone into sustainability and creating a place that will give London a real legacy.'

Perhaps the most vital transformation at the Olympic Park will be at the sports venues as they become part of the local community. As well as contributing to this new region of London, this transition will also help in fulfilling the promise to inspire more people to get involved with sport.

Whilst remaining a competition venue, the London 2012 Aquatics Centre – where USA swimmer Michael Phelps won his 22nd Olympic medal and became the most decorated Olympian of all-time and Tom Daley won his bronze medal in the men's Diving 10m Platform – is set to become one of the most impressive public swimming pools in the world.

Meanwhile, the VeloPark, home to the 6,000-capacity Velodrome – the stage for Team GB's incredible haul of seven Track Cycling gold medals – and a BMX track, will be open for visitors and will surely inspire London's ever-growing commitment to life on two wheels.

'It's a part of London that wasn't the most desirable place to live or to bring up a family,' said Hemingway. 'But all of a sudden, it's become this great place that kids and families will absolutely love. No kid could fail to be excited by the Olympic BMX track and all the other facilities that will become public.'

The London 2012 shop

Remember the Games with a fantastic selection of clothing, accessories, toys, books and more. From London 2012 shops or online at london2012.com/shop.

The 115m high Orbit is Britain's largest piece of public art

'It's an amazing opportunity to encourage young people to get involved and participate in sport'

Footballer and local lad David Beckham

The International Inspiration programme has reached 12 million children worldwide through sport

The Olympic Flag passes to Eduardo Paes, the Mayor of Rio de Janeiro, during the Closing Ceremony

'It is an amazing opportunity to encourage young people to get involved and participate in sport,' said Beckham, who grew up in the area. 'What better motivation than to have the world's greatest athletes performing on your doorstep?'

London 2012 has also inspired a number of other facilities outside the Olympic Park, all aimed at realising the ambition of encouraging more young people to take up sport. In 2008, adidas announced the creation of a number of multi-sport outdoor venues called 'adiZones', as part of a sports legacy initiative. With around fifty adiZones now installed in the UK, the venues are designed to encourage young people to be active and to create a legacy that lasts way beyond the London 2012 Games.

Earlier this year, Culture Secretary Jeremy Hunt unveiled a £1billion strategy to help honour London 2012's promise to inspire a generation to get involved in sport. The strategy, to be delivered by Sport England, will see every secondary school in England host new school-based sports clubs, that will be linked to one or more sports' national governing bodies.

As well as encouraging young people to take up sport, the initiative feeds into the legacy promise of making 'the UK a world-leading sporting nation' and producing a greater number of world-class athletes.

With Great Britain's record-breaking Olympic medal haul now secured, the London 2012 Games have undoubtedly inspired a generation of British athletes to succeed more than they ever have before. And for many of

Great Britain's upcoming elite athletes, London 2012 has already turned their focus to the next Olympic and Paralympic Games.

Whilst Britain's elite swimmers took to the pool at London 2012, the next generation of swimmers was heading to the US Open in Indianapolis. 'It will give them the chance to set new targets as they aim for the 2014 Commonwealth Games and beyond to Rio 2016,' said Mark Perry, British Swimming Development Coach.

'Within the development programme we have been looking at how we can bridge that gap by giving our younger swimmers the chance to compete at more high-quality senior meets, to make the transition easier.'

For British swimmer Russell Smith, the goal for the next four years is clear: 'London 2012 has had a massive impact in terms of exposure and coverage. This has made my desire to succeed even greater.'

So as the Olympic Flag was handed over to the Mayor of Rio de Janeiro at the Closing Ceremony of these Games, the attention now shifts to Rio 2016 and a new Olympic cycle begins.

And when the Olympic Cauldron is lit once again in Rio in four years' time, organisers will surely look to London, as the city that set the benchmark for how to deliver a real legacy.

London has successfully staged the world's greatest sporting event and its place in Olympic history has now been written. But as the world goes home, for London and the UK, the Games were just the preview.

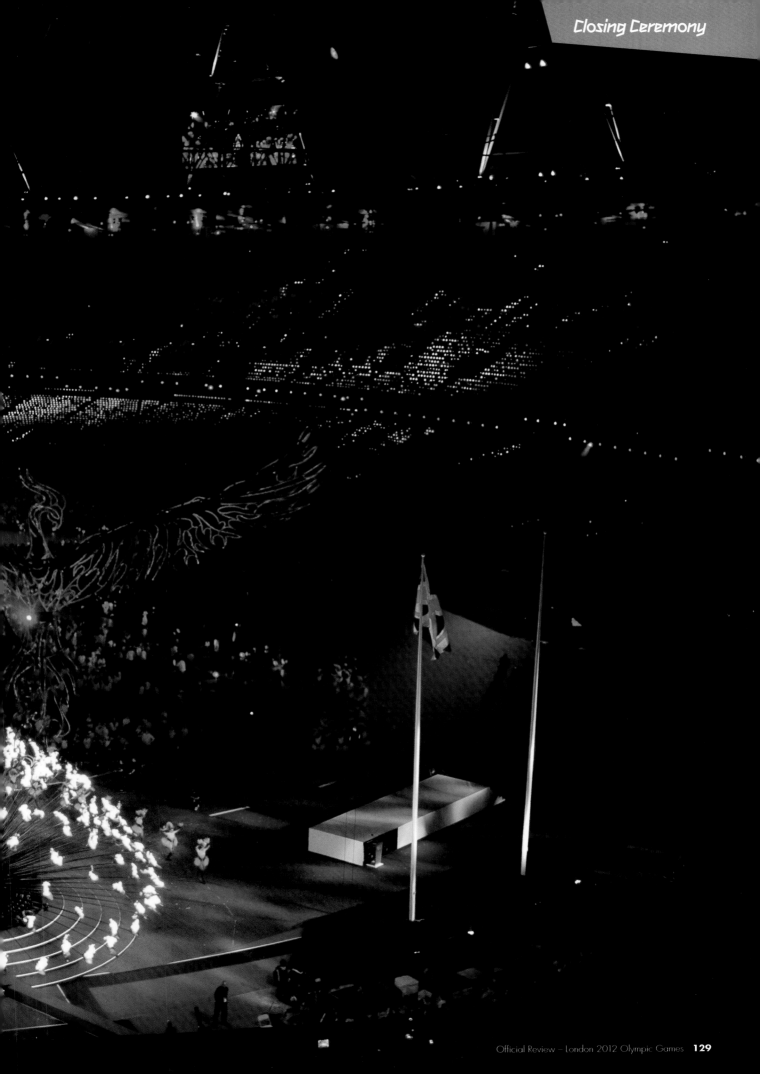